D1230606

PIN
POINTING
EXCELLENCE

**Visit www.pinpointingexcellence.com
for more information.**

bright sky press
HOUSTON, TEXAS

2365 Rice Boulevard, Suite 202,
Houston, Texas 77005

Copyright © 2011 by John Reed
No part of this book may be reproduced in any form or by any electronic or mechanical means,
including information storage and retrieval devices or systems, without prior written permission
from the publisher, except that brief passages may be quoted for reviews.

ISBN: 978-1-936474-17-2

10 9 8 7 6 5 4 3 2 1

Library of Congress Cataloging-in-Publication Data on file with publisher.

Editorial Direction, Lucy Herring Chambers
Creative Direction, Ellen Peeples Cregan
Design, Marla Garcia
Printed in Canada

The *TEC4* tool is in the early stages of development and use and as such does not meet the
guidelines for tests and measurements established by the American Psychological Association,
and it has not been normed to generate reliability and validity data.

PIN
POINTING
EXCELLENCE

The Key *to* Finding
a Quality
Executive Coach

John Reed PhD, MBA

bright sky press
HOUSTON, TEXAS

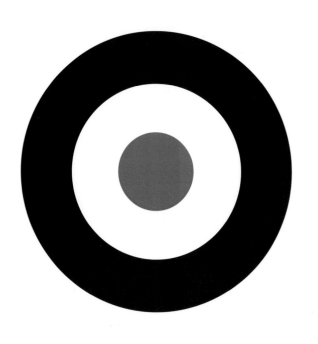

Table *of* Contents

INTRODUCTION:
Turning the Lights On **6**

CHAPTER 1
The Question of Quality **13**

CHAPTER 2
Start Taking Control.............................**35**

CHAPTER 3
Skirting Landmines.............................**55**

CHAPTER 4
Flexing Accurately **77**

CHAPTER 5
Final Cuts **93**

CHAPTER 6
Conclusion..**105**

APPENDIX **115**

First Response.................................... **116**

Bibliography **124**

Acknowledgements.............................**126**

Introduction:
Turning The Lights On

Why All the Fuss about Executive Coaches?

By any measure, I am most fortunate and privileged to work as an executive coach. I have trusting, confidential partnerships with exceptional clients and their organizations, and we expect that our work together will help them achieve their important goals. Executive coaching brings me satisfaction because I feel excitement when I help other people be more successful. I often learn more from my clients than I think they do from me, and I enjoy the friendship, support and collegiality of a number of the excellent executive coaches in the field.

I have serious concerns about the executive coaching field, however, as do many colleagues. I hope someday it will become a widely respected profession, but unless we become more proactive in shaping the definition of an executive coach, we won't meet that standard anytime soon. In terms of quality control, our field lags far behind many professions you and I count on every day. Valued service fields such as health care, law enforcement, education and the ministry have all established clear standards for admission, training, education and ongoing skill development. Executive coaching—with the potential to shape so many industries and affect so many people's employment experiences and productivity—has not.

Here's a common example: She may not be the foremost internal medicine practitioner in the world, but I know the physician I go to had to be smart, disciplined and dedicated enough to perform well in high school, graduate, perform well in college, graduate, earn admission to medical school, graduate, earn admission to an internship and residency, graduate, take board exams to be licensed by her state (Texas), pass them and, over time, continually educate herself to stay current in the field—just to receive and then to maintain a medical license, the ticket to work in her profession.

What does an executive coach need to do to earn the right to work in the field?

Absolutely nothing.

What training, experience, expertise and service quality can consumers be assured of when working with executive coaches?

None.

How long has the executive coaching field known about this situation?

Thirty years or more.

How have we as an industry responded to this situation?

"Not at all," say many familiar with executive coaching. "Very slowly and without coordination," say other, more optimistic observers.

So when can consumers realistically expect the executive coaching field to organize ourselves on at least a national—if not global basis? When can we set a single, clear set of requirements for education, training and ongoing development to ensure high service quality and consumer protection?

Again, answers from knowledgeable insiders and observers vary, from "Never" to a more optimistic "Not for decades."

So now what?

One option for me was to simply complain and criticize our field as loudly and persistently as possible. This of course would improve nothing.

Another option was to volunteer to help within the field to slowly move us towards organization. I could imagine this help would have value but, frankly, the rewards are akin to those of watching paint dry. I only wish I had that much patience.

The third option I saw was to work to equip consumers who buy our executive coaching services with tools and processes to help ensure top quality service and the highest returns on investment. This work has the value of putting power in the hands of those who deserve it—consumers—with the added benefit of providing the executive coaching field at large with a long overdue wake up call to organize itself.

I like Door #3, don't you? Before going through it, I wrestled with some questions, like who was I to put this information out for public consumption? Did my background qualify me to suggest how the entire field should be improved? The most pressing question, though, gave me the deciding answer: Would sharing my opinion be responsible and helpful?

Answering those questions for myself, I took inventory of what I have to share, with my clients and with others who might be interested in helping clarify the standards of executive coaching. I'm ethical, experienced and well-intentioned, at least. Pretty soon I'll reach the 20-year mark as an executive coach. About 30 years ago I finished business school and started work as an executive. I am fortunate to have had the chance to earn a Dartmouth MBA and a University of Georgia PhD, training that has since helped me as an executive, management consultant, licensed corporate psychologist and executive coach.

The bottom line is—I'm as qualified as I need to be in a field that lacks standards and I'm more experienced than most.

So, Where Do We Begin?

Recent estimates are that executive coaching is a growing, $2+ billion industry. Research in 2008 estimated conservatively that there were 50,000 executive coaches. In the near future that total will easily double. When executive coaching came into vogue about 30 years ago, global competition, advancing technology, rapid market and organizational shifts and other complicating factors were common. Business leaders started turning to executive coaches to help them determine how to function differently to be more effective.

In the early years, executive coaches focused their energy on clients who had ability but also self-defeating flaws. Today, instead of remedial support, executive coaches have the goal of helping outstanding, talented clients get the most from their abilities. These executives have excellent growth potential and want optimal performance and career development.

What's the Point of All This Analysis?

Being able to evaluate, select and use executive coaches as an even more savvy and discriminating consumer means you'll get top quality service and the best return on your coaching investment. Why is this important? Well, today's executive coaching marketplace provides a broad range of "executive coaches" offering a diverse set of services of widely-varying quality.

While facing this unsettling variation in quality, we also hear executive coaching called "an art and a science." The "art" element suggests that coaches are good at noticing subtleties in clients' personalities and ways of interacting with the world. These coaching skills are referred to as "intangible" and "hard to measure." This notion of subtle, non-quantifiable qualities combined with the confusing marketing messages many executive coaches generate can frustrate our effort to sensibly and systematically compare candidate coaches.

You're in a stronger position to cut through vague messages and to sift through this mass of candidates to identify a genuinely excellent coach when you use practical data and straightforward tools for uncovering vital information. You need to ensure that you select and use <u>only</u> the highest quality executive coaches, generating better returns on your outlay of time, energy and money.

In the next few chapters, I'm going to provide you with a process and tools for identifying a genuinely excellent coach with the proven abilities to make a difference.

Who Benefits from the Process?

If you are currently an executive coaching client or if you plan on hiring a coach in the near future, you need a practical and thorough approach for effectively and efficiently making apples to apples comparisons of executive coaches. Your result will be minimizing wasted time, money and energy and maximizing value you receive from coaching.

But having industry standards isn't just a client perk; it benefits everyone involved. If you're a leader responsible for developing prospective executive coaching clients, you'll experience more success when you provide quantifiably superior coaching talent to help your people realize their potential. The process I've developed will stimulate your thinking and common sense about executive coaches and their fit with your goals, making your selected coaches as impactful as possible.

If you're an HR professional or PEO provider, you're constantly analyzing when, if and with whom to apply executive coaching to best support your clients. With quantifiable data, you can carefully evaluate and compare executive coaches and provide a higher level of client satisfaction.

If you're on the faculty at a business school, you're trying to impress best practices upon your students. Having standards for executive coaches offers new perspectives and information for students researching executive coaching specifically as well as those seeking to understand the business world in general. Although at the moment there are few degree

9

programs in executive coaching at the masters or doctoral level, if you're an administrator building a graduate program in Executive Coaching, a thorough understanding of this process and these tools will prepare and position your graduates for success and credibility in the executive coaching market.

Perhaps most importantly, having a standard in executive coaching most benefits coaches who are interested in development. We can use this process and the questions put forth by the tools to get a baseline measure of our strengths and development opportunities, as young executive coaches or as experienced men and women who desire to continue to improve our field. With quantifiable assessment data, all of us can set obtainable goals and make plans for professional growth and personal development.

How Does It Work?

If you fall in to any of the aforementioned categories, you're always pressed for time. You need a process you can use efficiently. *Pinpointing Excellence* is lean, direct and short. On the last page of each chapter, I've provided a summary of that chapter's concepts. If you want to dig deeper, at the back, you'll find a bibliography of resources I find particularly compelling.

If you're a linear reader, dive in, and I'll meet you at the conclusion, where I hope you'll agree with me that this process will be an asset to people on both sides of the executive coaching relationship. But if you want to jump to a particular topic, here's what you'll find in the next pages:

Chapter 1: includes background data on executive coaching, its lack of organization and regulation, and your resulting need for clear, comparative information about coaches. Topics include a brief industry history, the absence of standards for education, experience and continuing training, an endless variety of coaches, wide variance in service quality, confusing marketing messages from coaches, unpredictable returns on your investments, and the unlikelihood that the executive coaching field will manage to coordinate internally to straighten itself out.

Chapter 2: introduces the idea that instead of you waiting for and depending on the executive coaching field to set high standards for professional training and service quality, you can help ensure that you get high quality executive coaching by using a quick, practical but rigorous process for evaluating and selecting coaches. It explains the selection tool, the *Top Executive Coach 4 (TEC4)*, used to evaluate a candidate coach's depth in business, psychology, coaching and ethics. The *TEC4* is easy to use, generating specific results to help you compare and contrast executive coaches.

Chapter 3: provides you with clarifying examples of using the *Top Executive Coach 4 (TEC4)*. You are introduced to familiar, prototypical characters you encounter in the executive coaching marketplace and how these characters are measured through the penetrating lens of the *TEC4*. The prototypical characters are also viewed through the lens of various "selection tips" offered in executive coaching literature. You see how the *TEC4* assessment is helpful in screening candidate coaches to make your "first cut" in the selection process.

Chapter 4: illustrates the versatility and flexibility you have in using the *TEC4* and the importance of applying your own values, experiences and priorities with the tool. You'll find several examples of how to tune the *TEC4* so that it incorporates your individual preferences. You can effectively and consistently grade coaching candidates and then focus on the top scorer(s), either using the *TEC4* in its standard format or in an adjusted format of your choice. This puts you in control so you can generate the most value.

11

Chapter 5: shows you how to generate more useful information about coaching candidates who made it to the top tier in Stage 1 of your evaluation and selection process. You'll be guided through Stage 2, the final stage of the process. You'll also find over 50 sample questions to use when interviewing candidates. These questions help you explore the strengths and weaknesses you identified using the *TEC4* in Stage 1 of selection. These questions also help you spot intangible characteristics by which you can further qualify and differentiate your candidates. You are in a strong decision-making position; you can weigh these intangible qualities clearly, without being distracted or confused by their subjective nature, because you rely first and foremost on your evaluation of more objective information about candidates in Stage 1.

Chapter 6: summarizes the preceding chapters and considers potential effects of using the recommended two-stage evaluation and selection process. Feedback from users of the system is summarized, and we make some conclusions. One conclusion is that, going forward, major improvements in executive coaching quality will be powered by individual decision-makers like you and not by the executive coaching industry itself. At the grass roots level, your well-informed decisions will drive up expectations and the need for coaches to raise our game. Collectively, you and fellow consumers will send a message that no executive coach can afford to ignore.

I've attempted to make it easy for you to refer back to the ideas here and—most importantly—to put them into practice. For example, the *Top Executive Coach 4 (TEC4)* is designed as a straightforward, practical and flexible tool, encouraging your quick ramp up the learning curve.

12

Appendices: there are eight appendices at the back of the book. They are offered to help you get rolling with the evaluation and selection process. You're welcome to reproduce or otherwise use this information as needed. However, since this information is proprietary, please have the following text appear legibly on each page, slide, or other form of material you distribute or otherwise use:

Copyright © 2011 by Dr. John L. Reed. All rights reserved.
www.pinpointingexcellence.com

The Question
of Quality

HERE'S ONE OF MANY WELL-ACCEPTED DEFINITIONS OF EXECUTIVE COACHING:

> *Executive coaching is a formal engagement in which a qualified coach works with an organizational leader in a series of dynamic, confidential sessions designed to establish and achieve clear goals that will result in improved business effectiveness, both for the individual and the organization.*

This definition sounds okay, right? It's short, to the point and reasonable. Unfortunately for you and other consumers of executive coaching, however, the most critical word in the above definition is also the most vague and undefined. That word is "qualified."

As an executive, you make your living by solving business problems. You evaluate possible solutions as thoroughly as possible before choosing and executing what you consider the best one. You want to be careful and thorough at work because your decisions can impact thousands or millions of dollars in revenue, costs or earnings together with the welfare of many employees.

So let's consider these points:

- Estimates are that $2 billion+ globally is spent each year on executive coaching
- Executive coaching has been in existence for at least 30 years
- Strangely, and in contrast with hundreds of other occupations, executive coaching has never had a single "entrance requirement;" no defined standards or expectations for an executive coach's education, training, experience, certification, licensure, continuous learning, etc.
- For decades, then, literally anybody could—and many have been—designating him or herself as "executive coach."
- The marketplace is now flooded with "executive coaches" of many backgrounds pitching their services and, each day, the flood waters keep rising

The irony of this situation is simply this:

Despite considerable training and experience in analytical thinking and decision-making, and the billions we spend on executive coaching, most of us in the executive community <u>do not</u> know how to accurately evaluate and select the best available executive coach from a group of candidates. Figuratively speaking, we have one hand tied behind our back as we jump in the boxing ring. We squint and hope perhaps to decipher our target through a thick, misty fog instead of confidently hitting the heart of it with a laser beam. I hope what you find here will help ensure your success in assessing and picking the best executive coach.

The Wild West

In the past few years you may have read an article in the *Harvard Business Review* titled "The Wild West of Executive Coaching." If you read it, you know that the article discusses the lack of discipline in executive coaching, noting that in the industry "barriers to entry are non-existent—many self-styled executive coaches know little about business and some know little about coaching." You should understand that the only thing everyone in the executive coaching industry agrees on is that there is not a single universally accepted standard for quality control and consumer protection. Buyers of executive coaching are always—and, many believe, increasingly—at risk.

In the US alone, executive coaching annual revenues exceed $1 billion (USD). This means thousands of businesspeople have bought or expect to buy services from an executive coach. The problem for these buyers (and perhaps for you) is that they don't know how to verify coaching quality and so assume—often incorrectly—that their executive coach is highly trained, deeply experienced, thoroughly educated and among the best in the field.

This problem is ridiculous and completely unnecessary. Before you buy almost any other professional service, you can verify qualifications. This quality control is available for—to name just a few—accountants, physicians, attorneys, psychologists, architects, financial planners, nurses and professors. When we're collectively spending hundreds of millions, why would we tolerate this ambiguity and absence of professional standards in providers of executive coaching?

We're smarter than that. We can do better. So let's proceed.

Executive Coaching Defined

The industry is so fragmented that no single description of executive coaching is endorsed universally. Here is a sampling of the many descriptions out there. You'll see that they have similarities but also a lot of variation.

- *Executive coaching is a formal engagement in which a qualified coach works with an organizational leader in a series of dynamic, confidential sessions designed to establish and achieve clear goals that will result in improved business effectiveness, both for the individual and the organization.*

- *Executive coaching is an experiential and individualized leader development process that builds a leader's capability to achieve short and long term organizational goals. It is conducted through one-on-one interactions, driven by data from multiple perspectives, and based on mutual trust and respect. The organization, an executive, and the executive coach work in partnership to achieve maximum impact.*

- *Executive coaching is a helping relationship formed between a client who has managerial authority and responsibility in an organization and a consultant who uses a wide variety of behavioral techniques and methods to assist the client to achieve a mutually identified set of goals to improve his or her professional performance and personal satisfaction and consequently to improve the effectiveness of the client's organization within a formally defined coaching agreement.*

- *Executive coaching provides one-on-one services to top-level leaders in an organization on the principle that positive changes can be leveraged to filter down and enhance the entire organization.*

- *Executive coaching is an approach to management—how one carries out the role of being a manager—and a set of skills for managing employee performance to deliver results.*

- *In executive coaching, psychological skills and methods are employed in a one-on-one relationship to help someone become a more effective manager or leader. These skills are typically applied to specific present-moment work-related issues (rather than general personal problems of psychopathology) in a way that enables the client to incorporate them into his or her permanent management or leadership repertoire.*

Thirty years ago, as a new business service, executive coaching faced questions including:

- How should an executive coach be trained and qualified to practice?
- What exactly is executive coaching?
- How does executive coaching differ from counseling, psychotherapy or mentoring?
- What is an executive coach responsible for providing to clients?

Rather than resolving these and other key issues to provide structure and to set solid professional standards, the executive coaching field spun its wheels. Some observers even believe we have regressed. In contrast to other fields that rightly call themselves "professions," executive coaching has yet to reach even these basic milestones:

17

- consensus-based global standards for admission to enter the field,
- consensus-based educational and training steps to qualify to practice in the field,
- consensus-based independent licensure or certification processes to demonstrate knowledge in the field,
- consensus-based continuing education requirements to maintain current knowledge in the field
- consensus-based mandatory ethical standards for serving executive coaching clients

Rolling the Dice—the Problem at Hand

"So what?" you may be thinking. What difference does all this make? Why should you bother reading about selecting high quality executive coaches?

One answer worth considering is that coaching is an unusually serious responsibility. The executives and organizations coaches work with provide them with sensitive information about, for instance, economics, corporate strategy, careers, anxieties, fears, doubts and plans. Clearly these corporations and their executives, families and communities can be enhanced or damaged depending on the quality of executive coaching they receive.

You won't be surprised at the second answer worth considering…money! As a consumer of executive coaching, you want to make your choice of a coach productive and successful. Rather than basing the determination mainly on the subjective feel of one or two short conversations or meetings with a candidate coach, you need the benefit of concrete, objective data to support your decisions.

If executive coaching were just a tiny cottage industry then the number of people receiving poor service from partially trained or untrained coaches would be small. Dissatisfied clients would be few and far between. Collectively, damage done to the business community and the circles it affects in the name of "executive coaching"—while unethical and embarrassing—would not be overwhelming.

Unfortunately, we know the opposite is true. Recent estimates are that in the US alone approximately $1 billion (USD) is spent on executive coaching. Already a sizable industry, it grows despite the absence of consumer protection and service quality control. Consequently, more decision makers are left hanging each day to select executive coaches unwisely and to suffer the consequences.

Some classic mistakes made in picking executive coaches include choosing a coach:

- unfamiliar with day to day business demands, corporate politics and organizational stressors existing in the client's setting
- lacking relevant training, education or certification in business, coaching, psychology or ethics
- following only one meeting or conversation
- based on unknowing, uninformed or unreliable references
- who makes unrealistic promises
- who lacks interpersonal skills
- who is prescriptive rather than inquiring—who claims to have all the answers yet is unskilled in helping clients find answers that work for them
- lacking psychological training to understand how and why each client thinks and operates differently from others—who is not able to help each client meet challenges in ways that make sense to him or her
- untrained and unlicensed in using psychological assessment tools
- inexperienced in executive management and leadership
- based on an attractive website
- lacking a strong, documentable track record
- lacking strong ethical grounding
- unaware of adult learning processes and dynamics
- from a positive first impression and enjoyable "chemistry"
- unable to plan and manage a coaching relationship over time
- lacking a proven approach or methodology
- before receiving a complimentary coaching session of 60-90 minutes

Ram Chamran, a coach to CEOs and other senior executives in the Fortune 100, comments in the *Harvard Business Review,* "The coaching industry will remain fragmented until a few partnerships build a brand, collect stellar people, weed out those who are not so good, and create a reputation for outstanding work."

In this fragmented market, to use Chamran's term, it is stunning to consider the volume of cash thrown away each year on what we mistakenly believe is high-quality executive coaching. This is a buyer beware scenario on a huge scale.

Caveat Emptor

When you need to find the best available executive coach, what does this all mean? You may need a coach, for example, to help one of your executives refine leadership skills to drive a new strategic project. The bottom line difference between success and failure in situations like this can mean tens or hundreds of million dollars for you. The stakes in making the right executive coaching choice are huge. Yet most buyers are not completely sure what to look for—and to insist on—in order to ensure excellent coaching results.

With so much riding on the quality of coach chosen, as we look into the executive coaching market, what confronts us?

- An unlimited variety of skill quality and levels of education, training and professional experience in people calling themselves an executive coach
- An unlimited variety of marketing and sales spins—noise generated by this huge population of coaches trying to make their way in the market
- A burgeoning number of definitions and categories of executive coaching itself

Each day for decades, anyone interested in proclaiming himself an executive coach did so. A number of these people have been ethical, well-meaning, compassionate, bright and eager to continuously build their skills through education and training. For each of these responsible professionals, however, there have been a number of charlatans, or wanna-bes. While other professions I've named operated with training, licensure, certification and other performance standards—to maintain service quality and to protect consumers—strangely, executive coaching left the barn door open to practitioners of any kind, from anywhere, at any time.

In the best of circumstances, we can spot these inadequate coaches by some tell-tale mistakes. Examples of these behaviors that are familiar to us include talking too much, only appearing to listen carefully, losing emotional control, and directing or encouraging something new without first ensuring the client is confident and psychologically prepared.

New executive coaches typically enter the market from three directions. The first and smallest group elects to go through an educational or certification process of some kind. The two larger groups are 1) retired or experienced executives aiming to share knowledge with the next generation and 2) people unsatisfied with their current careers or businesses who simply switch their title to coach.

21

Each executive coach, of course, then needs to practice a pitch—or "value proposition"—to promote services to the prospective client. With the rapidly increasing quantity and variety of executive coaches, the volume of marketing pitches is bewildering to many who listen to it and mind-numbing to the rest.

Speaking of pitches, below are a few classics. Notice how they can be confusing, contradictory, incomplete and of course self-serving? Heard any of these? Let's hope not.

- *I've always been a natural coach with a special, intuitive feel for people. I haven't bothered with formal training in business, psychology, coaching, ethics, etc. And, as proof of my natural giftedness, note that I've been doing my coaching for years.*
- *I actually worked as an executive so of course this quickly distinguishes me from other executive coaches. Training or experience in psychology, coaching, ethics and other areas isn't relevant*

since I've already been where my clients are.

- *Ethics in executive coaching would be valuable if I wasn't already a fine person.*
- *I'm not specially trained or educated (in—take your pick— psychology, business, coaching or ethics) but I work for (fill in the name of a business offering executive coaching) and they provide everything I need. Also, the fact that they hired me proves I'm talented.*
- *I've trained as a psychologist to see what's happening in the moment in working with clients. There's no substitute for this powerful insight so I don't need experience and education in additional areas like business or coaching.*
- *I sensed the coaching market changing—so I just completed a certification program of over 100 hours. I'm now a certified coach at the cutting edge of the field. Not every coach can say that—so who cares about depth in business or psychology?*

22

We can add more to this list but you get the point, right? In a nutshell: *All you (the consumer) need to know from me (the coach) is this—trust me, regardless of my actual training and experience, I'm well-prepared to work with you.*

Too Many Options

The book titled *The Art and Practice of Leadership Coaching: 50 Top Executive Coaches Reveal Their Secrets* identifies five types of executive coaching:

- Coaching Leaders / Behavioral Coaching
- Career / Life Coaching
- Coaching for Leadership Development
- Coaching for Organizational Change
- Strategy Coaching

For each of these five executive coaching types, ten respected coaches describe their unique approaches. Let's do the math. In this publication alone we're introduced to fifty sets of executive coaching styles, values, priorities, training, education and experience.

Similarly, another publication, *The Executive Coaching Handbook*, lists thirteen executive coaching categories:

- Personal / Life Coaching
- Career Coaching
- Group Coaching
- Performance Coaching
- Newly Assigned Leader Coaching
- Relationship Coaching
- High-Potential or Developmental Coaching
- Coaching to Provide Feedback Debriefing and Development Planning
- Targeted Behavioral Coaching
- Legacy Coaching
- Succession Coaching
- Presentation / Communication Skills Coaching
- Team Coaching

23

So, in addition to many differences between *individual coaches* in background, quality, training, experience, value propositions and methodologies, we appear to have over *a dozen categories* of executive coaching. Realistically, how could anyone not be confused?

Facing this confusion, the desire to cut to the chase to find the high quality service and performance needed is understandable. The chapters that follow will show you how to do just that, systematically and logically, to minimize unneeded irritation and to maximize your return on coaching dollars. You will be decidedly more comfortable and confident making decisions about hiring an executive coach when you know specifically what to look for and what to insist on for high quality.

It might seem counterintuitive that, after at least three decades, executive coaches are harder as opposed to easier to sort out and rate. Remember however that hundreds of practitioners of every background enter this industry each day without meeting a single admissions requirement. In the resulting turmoil, high quality is more elusive than ever as coaches accentuate assets and, just as importantly, downplay or distract us from their critical gaps in training, skill and experience.

Anne Scoular heads a global executive coaching firm. In the *Harvard Business Review* she notes that in picking an executive coach consumers should take into account whether the coach can describe clearly how he or she works with clients. She comments "If a prospective coach can't tell you exactly what methodology he uses—what he does and what outcomes you can expect—show him the door."

In light of Scoular's comments, the following assumption is reasonable: every executive coach needs training, skill and experience to develop an approach and in particular a methodology that is reliable and consistently effective. To put it another way, we can reasonably ask "How can a coach develop a reliable and effective methodology if he or she lacks fundamental, necessary qualifications for coaching?"

In Chapter 3 we'll look at this situation in more detail. For now, let's look at a prototypical executive coach, a fictional character we'll use for illustration.

Sam Smith

Sam just turned 40. He graduated from college and then worked in three organizations and three business functions (e.g. marketing, manufacturing, R&D) in the first 15 years of his career. From this experience, he learned that he is capable, bright and a people person—approachable and easy to talk with.

For any number of reasons, Sam decides to become an executive coach. He prints business cards, sets up a website, and looks for clients. He practices responses to the questions he knows will be coming. If you were his prospective coaching client, here's how a hypothetical exchange between the two of you might go. Let's listen carefully to what Sam is really saying.

You: Hi, Sam. Nice to meet you, and thanks for stopping by. I haven't had much experience with executive coaching. I did read a book called Pinpointing Excellence: The Key to Finding a Quality Executive Coach. *It said good executive coaching starts with strong training and experience in coaching and also in business, psychology and ethics. What could you share with me about your executive coaching background, philosophy and approach?*

Sam: *Well...you raise just the right points about how I became a strong coach. I've been lucky to be able to draw from 15 years of executive experience in different business disciplines to help my fellow executives, folks like you, perform better and have more success.*

Reading between the lines, what can you take away from Sam's answer?

Sam does not have an executive coaching "philosophy" beyond what he just said to you. He hasn't had a chance to acquire training or experience in executive coaching. He's not qualified to use psychological assessment instruments, among other analytical tools. He's a rookie, but he has to start somewhere.

You: I'd imagine with your experience as an executive coach, Sam, you see lots of people like me—people who want to make changes, to communicate and behave differently, to progress further in their career. So going back to your training and experience, I'm sure your years in business must be valuable in what you do. Do you have graduate training in business? An MBA? And what program did you graduate from? Could I see a transcript?

Sam: I've learned a tremendous amount from my own executive experience. I've developed as a professional over many years and worked through a number of tough challenges—like many I'll bet you've faced. This gives me a unique edge, a special appreciation and empathy for executives I work with who are sharp and motivated to succeed. I considered business school but was enjoying success without it.

One possible translation here is that Sam's business training is entirely on-the-job.

You: I appreciate that you have many years of executive experience, Sam. Your work history sounds impressive. Could I see a copy of your resume, please? My friends and colleagues who have had coaching tell me it involves change, sometimes pretty demanding change. I'm sure your clients go through changes in working with you. You must understand this area well. What's your training and experience in areas like behavior change, adult development and psychology?

Sam: I often reflect back on many challenges, changes and the resulting growth I experienced during my business career. You're right, it is really important to know firsthand what it takes to stretch and develop to be more successful. I agree with you—this has been a key in my own growth and in the growth my clients achieve in our work together.

Sam's deflection of the question suggests he isn't trained in adult development, psychological assessment or related subjects that he could draw on to help his coaching clients succeed in changing behavior and then in maintaining those changes.

You: So if I understand correctly, you're saying that you've been successful without training in psychology. You must be very capable—a natural at this—right, Sam? Interesting. Well, let's move on. Again, not being an expert on coaching, I checked a couple of coaching websites. There are several. One was for the Worldwide Association of Business Coaches and another was for the International Coach Federation. Apparently certification is becoming more widespread and important for executive coaches. Do you belong to a coaching organization, Sam? What was the certification process like for you? How has it helped you in working with clients? Could I see a copy of your certification document(s) please?

Sam: *Thanks very much. I appreciate the compliment about my background and experience as a coach. Again, you're absolutely right. There's no substitute for executive experience when it comes to executive coaching. So I've found it unnecessary to go through a formal process. That's the advantage of being a seasoned executive, I suppose. I recommend those coaching programs to folks I know who are interested in coaching but have no real business experience. In my case, knowing so much already about what executives really face, courses wouldn't help much. I've been lucky enough to have good results in working with a number of clients. I'll refer you to these people so you get a sense of how we worked together and what we accomplished. OK?*

Sam's trying to deflect you from the issue of his executive coaching education and training—since he has none. He's also trying to obscure or minimize the value of meeting coaching certification standards and, instead, to put you in touch with people who, for any number of reasons—including that they may not know of executive coaching that's any better—would say good things about his work.

You: *I've been told coaching can be really sensitive, personal work. It sounds like my coach and I would wrestle with a lot of stuff I don't usually talk about. I'm a little nervous about that. Things like trust, confidentiality and ethics mean a lot to me. How do you feel about these issues in working with clients, Sam? What ethics code do*

27

you operate under, and may I have a copy of it please?

Sam: *I couldn't agree with you more. Ethics are tremendously important. I come from a good family and was brought up with strong values. I'm sure you were, too. My work with clients is of course based on high standards of trust and respect. I hold what clients talk about in confidence, certainly. I've never had problems there. Again, I'll be happy to provide references for you.*

Sam's not operating under an ethics code and does not have a copy of one. So, he can't provide you with a clear ethical picture of your rights and his obligations during the executive coaching relationship.

Get the Picture?

The preceding dialogue simply illustrates a bit of the marketing clutter consumers of executive coaching have to wade through. Unfortunately, the dialogue may sound familiar to you. Conversations like this happen every day as consumers try to decide about coaches with vague, incomplete or irrelevant information.

Let's give Sam credit. His answers have an encouraging tone. He's a nice guy and a people person. He develops rapport and makes others feel comfortable. He conveys a positive outlook and delivers upbeat pep talks.

We cannot fault him for trying to sell what he has to sell. He highlights his business background, correctly suggesting how his executive experience helps in working with executive clients.

You'll notice that Sam *only* talks about business experience, however. We see that he's a one-trick pony. Knowing this, he tries to steer the conversation around key facts such as his lack of graduate training in business or psychology, training and certification in coaching, and accountability to a formal code of ethics.

We can commend Sam for doing his best with what he has. If you don't know better (and usually consumers don't) it's easy to simply enjoy the warmth of Sam's company and not evaluate him

THE KEY TO FINDING A QUALITY EXECUTIVE COACH

thoroughly. But if you then chose Sam and he starts working with you, you could also be in the painful position of not knowing how to assess the quality of his service or to track any progress you make as a result of it.

Sooner or later you'll wonder if anything useful is being offered. When it dawns on you that you've been working with a coach who is not fully trained, you—quite correctly—will be angry. You'll spread the news about the executive coach who was ineffective and failed to meet your expectations. You'll suffer, of course, as will your organization—valuable money and time down the drain.

Coaching Certification: The Merry-Go-Round

The optimistic outlook is that recent steps to certify coaches signal progress in the industry. For example, certification standards have been set by organizations such as the Worldwide Association of Business Coaches (WABC) (www.wabccoaches.com), the International Association of Coaches (IAC) (www.certifiedcoach.com), the International Coach Federation (ICF) (www.coachfederation.org), the Association for Coaching (www.associationforcoaching.com) and the European Mentoring and Coaching Council (www.emccouncil.org).

Consumers have started noticing certification efforts. The U.S. government, for example, has started mandating in Request for Proposal (RFP) documents that executive coaches be certified by the ICF.

As the user of executive coaching, you may find this encouraging. Not everyone applauds this progress in setting quality standards, however. If you look closely, it will become clear that most executive coaches still lack certification of any kind. Not surprisingly, only 29% of coaches polled in a Harvard Business Review survey indicated it was very important to be certified in a proven coaching method.

The Question of Quality

I'm in no way advocating or endorsing one coaching organization (e.g. WABC, IAC, ICF, etc.) with credentialing processes in place over another. Organizations in this category identify themselves to us as leaders in the industry, working to set performance and quality standards and to promote knowledge-sharing among member coaches.

We should acknowledge contributions of these and similar organizations. Slowly, in the turbulent executive coaching market, minimal—but not yet mandatory—quality standards are being established to raise the bar for everyone in the equation's benefit. We may hope these standards become much more stringent but, for the moment, the fact that they are gaining public acceptance is positive.

For example, International Coach Federation (ICF) certification at one level—called the Associate Certified Coach (ACC) level—is earned with approximately 130 hours of coursework, 50 documented hours of coaching experience, demonstrated understanding of ICF core competencies, adherence to ICF ethical standards, and letters of recommendation from ICF—certified coaches. These requirements pale in comparison to, say, a four year post-doctoral medical internship and residency following four tough years of medical school. However, they are at least a first line of defense for consumer protection and service quality control.

We of course want these early certification efforts to gain momentum. They represent the start of the executive coaching industry organizing into a profession consumers can rely on. You might expect executive coaches in greater numbers to work toward certification and, indeed, many are.

We should hold off on our celebrations, however, for the following reason. Many of the thousands of uncertified executive coaches in the marketplace are pushing back. For example, three global consulting firms offering executive coaching services are concerned about being required in situations such as Request for

Proposal documents from the U.S. government to verify that their coaches are certified by the International Coach Federation (ICF.)

Rather than have their coaches get in line and earn ICF certification, these three firms are now considering forming their own proprietary standards and processes so they can then mount arguments—with the federal government, for instance—that they should be able to certify their own executive coaches and that their coaches will then be sufficiently certified.

Let's assume for the moment that this consortium of three firms moves ahead as anticipated. We would expect that another set of certification standards would emerge. Then you might well ask "How will the rest of the providers of executive coaching react?"

Other providers could react three ways. They could 1) arrange for their coaches to earn the currently accepted certification from ICF; 2) arrange—if possible—for their coaches to earn the new certification from their direct competitors, the consortium of three firms or, most likely, 3) form *their* own processes and standards for certification.

In short order, then, we could witness individual consulting firms and corporations of executive coaches try to be self-appointing and self-certifying, just as individual executive coaches have been doing for decades. Instead of becoming more ordered, the field would be increasingly chaotic.

If every individual and organization sets proprietary quality or certification standards, do you think there can ever be an independently-maintained, reliable, single global standard for quality? Certainly not. And, if not, we're doomed to face more risk and confused decision-making, with even more unsatisfactory outcomes.

While we're on this subject, let's acknowledge that the value of certification in coaches is being diluted another way. Organizations like WABC, IAC and ICF can set certification requirements, for example, to include over 100 hours of training. In contrast, those of us signing into our LinkedIn (www.linkedin.com) account early in

2011 saw the following message scroll across the top of the page:

> *Be a Certified Coach—$979—Earn your credentials in 16 hours in our highly interactive and fun course.*

Certification in 16 hours? Why not 8 hours or, for that matter, 45 minutes? In all seriousness, how do we benefit as consumers of "certified executive coaching" if this designation gives no dependable assurance of quality?

The Right Step Forward

Few of us actually expect the executive coaching industry to become focused on setting and enforcing independent global standards for qualification, admission, training, licensure or certification. On the contrary, we are realizing that it is up to us as consumers and motivated practitioners to improve coaching service quality by setting our own high standards. If you're taking the time to read this book, you've probably wanted to take this initiative—or see it happen—but may have lacked all the information and support you need to do so.

It is reasonable—and high time—for us to insist on practical, apples-to-apples evaluations of executive coaches. It is the only way to be assured of excellent results for your coaching investment. In support of this goal, the next chapter introduces a straightforward way to objectively sort through executive coaches.

RECAP—CHAPTER 1

- Executive coaching is a 30+ year old, global, fragmented and disorganized industry, now estimated at $2+B annually.

- There are no standards or entrance requirements to become an executive coach—in education, experience, certification, licensure, continuous learning, ethical conduct or service quality.

- Since 1980, at least, anyone interested in using the label "executive coach" could do so with no questions asked. The marketplace, referred to as "The Wild West" by many, is packed with executive coaches of widely varying quality, education, training and experience.

- Despite spending large sums of money on executive coaching and desiring to select the best quality coaches, most executives do not have a system for fully and accurately screening candidate coaches and selecting the most effective one.

- A hypothetical conversation with a fictional executive coach, Sam Smith, provides a sample of the confusing or misleading marketing messages that many consumers have to wade through.

- A number of coaching organizations (e.g. Worldwide Association of Business Coaches (WABC), Association for Coaching (AC), International Coach Federation (ICF), European Mentoring and Coaching Council (EMCC), and International Association for Coaches (IAC)) are commendable in working to establish certification standards for executive coaches. However, their efforts meet with strong push-back since most executive coaches are not certified and do not seek to be certified.

- Consumers and motivated practitioners have waited for decades for the executive coaching industry to organize and create one set of strong global standards. Looking forward, there is no clear evidence of a solution coming anytime soon.

- However, we are not doomed to the "same-old-same-old." We can improve the quality of executive coaching and our return on investment by evaluating coaches in a straight-forward, rigorous and practical way that will be introduced in Chapter 2.

2

Start Taking Control

DESPITE HUGE FINANCIAL OUTLAYS FOR EXECUTIVE COACHING, THE REALITY IS THAT MANY CONSUMERS DO NOT FULLY UNDER-STAND THE STRENGTHS, development needs and overall background of the executive coach they nevertheless pick. On both sides of the equation, we may lack data necessary to set higher expectations for coaches. Many of us don't realize how much better our coaching results could be.

Choosing Too Quickly

Why do so many of us continue working with a lack of key information, making sub-optimal coaching choices? Part of the answer may be in the hurried steps sometimes taken to locate and evaluate coaches.

Picture, for instance, that you need an excellent coach for yourself or one of your key executives. You or your firm may be aware of some coaches and may search on line for others. You may call friends and colleagues to ask them about the coaches they use. Pretty quickly, coaches familiar to your firm, recommended by others, and/or uncovered via Google searches are invited to interview. So far, so good.

Usually each coach visits with the person to be coached and with an executive from, say, human resources or talent management for an hour or less. The candidate's background is discussed for a few minutes, expectations are reviewed, and first impressions— good or bad—are formed. Then the executive to be coached thinks through the meetings with the candidate coaches, tests his thinking with the colleague from human resources or talent management, and decides on a coach.

When asked why they selected a coach, reasons for the final decision are typically that the selected coach "was easy to get along with," "seemed good to work with" and "just felt right." Comfort or "fit" is critical. This makes sense. We all want to be comfortable in our relationships, and the executive coaching relationship usually lasts several months or more.

Sometimes, against the odds, this process actually works and produces a top quality coach, if the coach making a nice first impression happens also to be the most talented. There is no correlation, however, between the quality of the first impression made by a coach and his or her effectiveness.

Here's a second popular approach to matching client with coach: Your organization—the human resources department in particular—already knows an executive coach, is comfortable with the coach, and arranges for the coach to work with you.

This is fine if, in the beginning, the coach was carefully

evaluated in comparison to other available coaches. Of course, if the selection process first used to pick the coach was loose and subjective, your company may have settled unknowingly for less than top talent and now, not realizing the error, continues living with the first decision.

What's Missing?

The steps described above are a good start for thinking about different coaches. To maximize our odds of picking a star and not a lemon, however, we need to strengthen them. Let's look at the facts. We have very little information about how the coaches in the previous examples compare in critical, objective areas such as depth of training, experience, education, etc. in coaching, business, psychology and ethics.

In subjective areas, what do we know about how they stack up in intellect, emotional qualities, interpersonal skills, self-awareness, or working styles? As we incorporate this kind of additional knowledge into the selection process for executive coaches our batting average goes up.

37

Boosting Quality

Since every executive coach has a value proposition, there are lots of pitches coming at you and other decision-makers. You can expect to receive conflicting messages about what executive coaching is and about what competencies and characteristics are important in executive coaching. You need to eliminate confusion and increase coaching quality by taking practical, logical steps to zero in on the best candidate.

Anyone experienced in working with senior business leaders trusts these assumptions:

- KISS (Keep It Simple Stupid)
- Valuable solutions are usually straightforward, practical,

metrics based, logical and rooted in common sense.
- Psychobabble, coachese and consulting buzz-words are counterproductive.
- While tangible, reliable markers of professional training and experience do not guarantee success, they do maximize the likelihood of excellent preparation which, in turn, maximizes the likelihood of success

Useful vs. Fundamental

As a first step in clarifying what is most important, let's consider the hundreds of qualities and skills typically described as *useful* in executive coaches. Here's a small fraction of that list:

> ….*assertiveness, openness, flexibility, goal orientation, partnering, continuous learning, integrity, facilitating development, promoting change, maturity, self-confidence, positivity, energy, interpersonal sensitivity, multicultural awareness, contracting, development planning, influencing, aligning, allying, transitioning, inquiring, trustworthiness, approachability, political savvy, curiosity, self-awareness, delegation, confrontation, giving feedback, goal-setting, training, reinforcement, active listening, time management, meeting management, problem-solving, conflict resolution…and on and on.*

We could argue that every characteristic on the list is *useful* in work as an executive coach. For that matter, we could also argue that every characteristic on the list is useful in dozens of occupations besides coaching.

So the list helps us but does not clarify for us exactly what is *fundamental and necessary* (vs. useful) for excellence in executive coaching. The list could do more to help us distinguish the relative importance of one characteristic versus another. We could then be more precise in using the list to evaluate, rank and pick a top executive coach.

The Vagueness of Art

We sometimes hear executive coaching called "an art and a science." The art element suggests coaches have valuable, hard—(if not impossible)—to—measure skills in noticing subtleties in clients and in their interactions with clients. Coaches have these skills in different combinations, which we'll talk more about in Chapter 5.

Since these skills incorporate intangible concepts and processes, they often do not help us rigorously compare coaches. The notion of subtle, indefinable or non-measurable qualities in executive coaches, combined with the confusing marketing messages executive coaches generate, can frustrate our effort to make intelligent buying decisions by sensibly and systematically evaluating candidate coaches.

Being "non-measurable" is convenient and helpful for coaches who are best served by staying below our radar, in the smoky land of intangibles, where their questionable qualifications and skills are hard for us to nail down. Coaches in this group are often the first to claim that executive coaching competence is complex and impossible to tie to experience, training or education. It is not surprising to us that coaching looks viable to almost anyone. Not many $2+ billion markets offer this kind of hiding place for less than fully-qualified practitioners.

From Confusion to Clarity

There indeed *are* differences in value and relative importance among the many useful executive coaching qualities and competencies. When we know what is most important to target, we can progress from the one extreme of buyer confusion and no industry standards to:

- Making consistent, thorough comparisons and rankings of executive coaches

- Revealing specific strengths and gaps in an executive coach's background
- Lowering odds of using mediocre to bad coaching, and the resulting wasted resources
- Sharing information and collectively raising service quality
- Freeing us from relying on the executive coaching field to organize itself
- Providing specific, constructive feedback to coaches, citing strengths to build on and opportunities for development
- Weeding out the highly variable market; voting with our dollars to get only the best

Four Fundamentals

Criteria to use to evaluate coaches fall into two categories: *fundamental*—which I'll introduce here and delve further into in Chapters 3 and 4—and *useful*—discussed further in Chapter 5. Based on my experience and common sense, there are four fundamental "must have" areas for excellence in executive coaching:

Business Depth
Psychology Depth
Coaching Depth
Ethics Depth

Fundamental #1: Business Depth

Experience, training and knowledge in business and management may sound like a no-brainer to us for any coach working with corporations and their executives. Yet, believe it or not, there are thousands of executive coaches with little to no foundation in this area.

Here are just a few business topics for executive coaches to be grounded in:

- Management principles, processes and best practices
- Leadership principles, processes and best practices
- Organizational design and development processes and best practices
- Deep, industry-specific expertise
- Governance principles, processes and best practices
- Functional areas (e.g. finance, marketing) and their interdependencies
- Corporate board management
- Talent management and succession planning
- Merger and acquisition issues
- Onboarding into new roles or assignments
- Information technology developments and processes
- Reengineering and downsizing
- Diversity management
- Human resource management
- Distinctions between profit and not-for-profit organizations and operations

Where and how would an executive coach acquire this know-how? Here are typical channels:

- Substantive work experience as an executive
- Undergraduate and/or graduate education in business
- Continuous training in business

Straight forward, right? Let's move to the next fundamental.

Fundamental #2: Psychology Depth

For a coach working with intelligent, achievement oriented and complex executives, there is no substitute for understanding how and why each client thinks and behaves differently. Top coaches get a sense of the client's perspective and situation. Consequently they can help the client diagnose his or her challenges and resolve them.

Executive coaches with psychology depth are also helpful in working with the client to make sense of psychological issues that can be the source of business performance issues. For example, a psychologist who studies executives and workplace issues, Dr. Steven Berglas, cites narcissism as one such issue.

Dr. Berglas says, "It is not all that uncommon to find narcissists at the top of workplace hierarchies; before their character flaws prove to be their undoing, they can be very productive. Narcissists are driven to achieve, yet because they are so grandiose, they often end up negating all the good they accomplish. Not only do narcissists devalue those they feel are beneath them, but such self-involved individuals also readily disregard rules they are contemptuous of."

Of course we understand that even the most skilled executive coach is not necessarily trained as a clinical psychologist to treat narcissism and other psychological issues. Understanding and recognizing these issues, however, positions the coach to act responsibly—at least in helping the client locate the psychotherapeutic support needed and adjusting the executive coaching program accordingly.

Often psychologists are trained to recognize and understand narcissism and other personality disorders as a type of mental illness marked by unhealthy and rigid patterns of thinking and behaving. Personality disorders lead to interpersonal or relationship issues at work and home. Recognizing and understanding these disorders is critical in executive coaching because recent research from the Academy of Management (AOM) indicates that almost 1 in every 5 working adults (18% of men, 16% of women) has or has had at least one personality disorder.

Here are just a few areas of psychological knowledge and skill needed by executive coaches:

- Assessing personality, leadership styles, problem-solving skills and other executive characteristics using reliable and valid tools and methods of psychological assessment
- Accessing, understanding, applying and producing research on personality, emotion, career development, stress management, behavioral change, adult learning, individual and group behavior, gender differences, emotional intelligence, and related topics relevant in the executive community

Executive coaches would gain this and related knowledge through:

- Experience working as a psychologist or related professional (e.g. psychiatrist, counselor)
- Undergraduate and/or graduate education and training in psychology
- Continuous education and training in psychology

43

There's a pattern here.

Fundamental #3: Coaching Depth

You and I understand that, obviously, executive coaches need experience and training in coaching. We expect executive coaches to take full advantage of educational and training opportunities available in coaching, since these are currently limited. It seems absurd then that there are thousands of executive coaches with no education or training in coaching.

As we discussed earlier, the executive coaching field is only starting to institute options for graduate education and training. There is only a handful of graduate level coaching programs, compared with many for psychological or management training. For example, the Worldwide Association of Business Coaches (WABC) offers a Master of Arts degree in Professional Development (Business Coaching).

We hear about coaching certification programs—shorter, lighter-weight education and training in coaching than what graduate level programs offer—that are in good supply. For example, WABC-approved coaching programs are available from The Excel Centre, the Direct Selling Women's Alliance and the Meyler Campbell Business Coach Program. Examples of ICF-approved coaching programs include The College of Executive Coaching, Georgetown University, and iCoachNewYork.

As consumers, it's reasonable to assume executive coaches educate themselves via graduate level and/or certification programs and have substantial knowledge and skill in a number of coaching subjects such as:

- Differentiating executive coaching from other forms of coaching
- Staying current with shifts and developments in the practice of executive coaching
- Understanding and applying models and theories of executive coaching
- Understanding the impact in executive coaching on the client, the client's organization, and the coach

Executive coaches would gain this and related knowledge through:

- Experience working as an executive coach
- Undergraduate and/or graduate education and training in coaching
- Education and training in coaching via reputable certification programs
- Continuous education and training in coaching

Not surprised are you?

Fundamental #4: Ethics Depth

Executive coaches work with clients who are vulnerable. They need support, and they're often unable to track the quality of coaching service they receive. It is critical to have the assurance that our executive coaches operate under a well-defined and published code of ethics. It is equally important to be able to count on our coaches maintaining an up-to-date understanding of ethical issues and practices for the industry.

Ethics depth in coaches is also critical because clients—as executives—are increasingly evaluated by their organizations based on ethics, integrity and related aspects of character. Sophisticated, forward-thinking models of executive leadership have character as a key element. An acknowledged cutting edge firm in this area, for instance, is Leadership Worth Following, LLC (www.worthyleadership.com). Increasingly, both executives and their coaches are expected to model and be governed by sound ethical practices.

A number of organizations publish ethical codes and guidelines for coaches to use to build knowledge. For example, the Academy of Management (AOM) ethics code is helpful for coaches with an executive background. The American Psychological Association (APA) ethics code helps coaches who are also psychologists. Ethical guidelines specifically for coaches are available from many sources such as WABC and ICF.

Executive coaches would gain this and related knowledge by:

- Joining an organization(s) (e.g. AOM, APA, WABC) with a published ethics code
- Studying and otherwise familiarizing themselves with the ethics code(s)
- Gaining experience in applying the ethics code(s) in client situations
- Maintaining, executing and documenting a plan for continuous education and training in ethics

The Fundamentals in Action

Since depth in business, psychology, coaching and ethics are prerequisites for excellent executive coaching, the next step is to start using these four fundamental areas to distinguish among coaches. I'll start by describing the *Top Executive Coach 4 (TEC4)*, the diagnostic tool we will be using.

The Top Executive Coach 4 (*TEC4*)

The *TEC4* is an original tool to help consumers make an informed "first cut" in Stage 1 of our evaluation process in choosing a coach. Later, in Chapter 5, we'll discuss Stage 2 of the evaluation process and how to help buyers make the "final cut." The *TEC4* is valuable in Stage 1 of our selection process as a checklist, grading sheet and snapshot of strengths and development areas.

The *TEC4* provides a scoring range for your coach of 0-25 points for each of the four fundamental categories (Business Depth, Psychology Depth, Coaching Depth, and Ethics Depth). Our hypothetical perfect executive coach earns 100 points.

Think back to your school days when 90-100 points earned an A, 80-89 earned a B, 70-79 earned a C, and on down the scale. *TEC4* scores help you identify the highest scorers, make your first cut, and then move your highest scorer(s) on to the second selection phase.

Here is the standard *TEC4* worksheet:

1. Business Depth
- Applied Experience   0-10 points   ____
- Education & Training   0-10 points   ____
- Continuous Development   0-5 points   ____

2. Psychology Depth
- Applied Experience   0-10 points   ____
- Education & Training   0-10 points   ____
- Continuous Development   0-5 points   ____

3. Coaching Depth
- Applied Experience   0-10 points   ____
- Education & Training   0-10 points   ____
- Continuous Development   0-5 points   ____

4. Ethics Depth
- Business Ethics Code   0-5 points   ____
- Psychology Ethics Code   0-5 points   ____
- Coaching Ethics Code   0-15 points   ____
- **TOTAL**   0-100 points   ____

Categories and Items Explained

The *TEC4* is straightforward and simple to use. For each of the four categories (e.g. Business Depth) we are provided with three *items* (e.g. Applied Experience, Education & Training, and Continuous Development).

As we start using the *TEC4*, our first question is usually how to assign points or "grade" the items. The following is a recommended approach for you to use in assigning points. In Chapter 4 I'll provide examples of adjusting this approach, if you find this flexibility helpful. For the moment, let's start with the basic approach.

Here are the twelve *TEC4* items and their scoring ranges:

1. Applied Experience (Business)(0—10 points):

Unquestionably, on the job business experience has value for executive coaches. We can estimate this value based on both the quality and quantity of the coach's experience. The quality of business experience can be graded based on factors such as the coach's level of responsibility, size of company, number of reports, etc. The quantity of the coach's executive experience is measured in years.

- 20+ yrs. of top quality experience   10 points
- 20+ yrs. of solid quality experience   8-9 points

- 11-19 yrs. of top quality experience   6-7 points
- 11-19 yrs. of solid quality experience   5 points
- 5-10 yrs. of top quality experience   4 points
- 5-10 yrs. of solid quality experience   3 points
- 1-4 yrs. of top quality experience   2 points
- 1-4 yrs. of solid quality experience   1 point

2. Education & Training (Business) (0—10 points)

We can think of the spectrum of business education and training having, at one end, highly selective MBA programs that are consistently ranked in the global Top 25 by, for example, the *Financial Times.* This group would include such programs as Wharton, London Business School, Harvard, Insead, Stanford, IE Business School, Tuck (Dartmouth), IIMA, IMD and HEC Paris. The next category includes selective MBA programs with global rankings at #26 or below. Next are essentially non-selective MBA programs, in which most anyone with a check can enroll. Next are bachelor's programs in business. The final category includes business courses offered through an associate degree program. Scoring would be:

- Top 25 MBA Program   9-10 points
- Selective MBA Program   7-8 points
- Non-selective MBA Program   5-6 points
- Bachelor's Degree Program   2-4 points
- Associate's Degree Program   0-1 points

3. Continuous Development (Business)(0-5 points):

With documented evidence of attending and completing seminars, executive education programs, continuing education courses, etc. give the coach 5 points. What's particularly important is evidence of regular and consistent learning. If learning has been occasional, perhaps assign 2-3 points. Without documented evidence, don't give the coach any points.

4. Applied Experience (Psychology) (0-10 points):

The *TEC4* ranks the coach's quality of psychological experience based on post-graduate work that is practical and applied (i.e. working with clients) rather than academic or research based, since coaching services are, likewise, applied. Scoring would be:

• 20+ yrs. of top quality experience	10 points
• 20+ yrs. of solid quality experience	8-9 points
• 11-19 yrs. of top quality experience	6-7 points
• 11-19 yrs. of solid quality experience	5 points
• 5-10 yrs. of top quality experience	4 points
• 5-10 yrs. of solid quality experience	3 points
• 1-4 yrs. of top quality experience	2 points
• 1-4 yrs. of solid quality experience	1 point

5. Education & Training (Psychology)(0-10 points):

As with business management education, we can consider the selectivity, rigor and ranking of the coach's academic program and work in psychology or a related field like psychiatry or counseling. Consider whether the coach earned a bachelors, masters or doctoral degree, and where. Following training, did the coach go on to earn licensure or board certification by passing relevant national exams? Consequently, how well prepared do you think the coach is to understand, diagnose and support processes of, for example, behavior change, learning and adult development that are critical in executive coaching. Scoring would be:

49

• Doctoral degree, licensure Top 25 program	10 points
• Doctoral degree, licensure selective program	8-9 points

- Doctoral degree, licensure
  non-selective program   6-7 points
- Master's degree,
  Top 25 program   5 points
- Master's degree,
  selective program   4 points
- Master's degree,
  non-selective program   3 points
- Bachelor's degree program   1-2 points
- Associate's degree program   0-1 points

6. **Continuous Development (Psychology)(0- 5 points):**
   Any coaches who are doctoral-level, licensed psychologists
   are responsible for regular continuing education to maintain
   their psychology license. With documented evidence of regular attendance in continuing education courses, etc. to satisfy
   professional licensure requirements, assign the coach 5 points.
   Without documented evidence of continuing education and
   maintenance of licensure, assign no points.

7. **Applied Experience (Coaching)(0-10 points):**
   WABC, IAC, ICF and other reputable firms offering coaching certification programs require coaches to document
   and report coaching hours. Documented hours count, in
   contrast with simple claims by a coach of "years of experience" or "hundreds of hours of work with clients" that are
   undocumented. Reputable firms can provide a coach with
   letters or forms confirming total coaching hours. Ask for
   this documentation.

- 2000+ documented coaching hours   10 points
- 1500+ documented coaching hours   8-9 points
- 1000+ documented coaching hours   6-7 points
- 500+ documented coaching hours   4-5 points
- 1+ documented coaching hours   0-3 points

8. Education & Training (Coaching)(0-10 points):

As mentioned earlier, education and training options to pursue in this category are limited, based on our current available data. Coaches can choose from a small number of master's level graduate programs in coaching and a wider variety of coaching certification programs. Remember that the quality of programs varies. Scoring would be:

- Master's degree accredited program   10 points
- Quality certification
  (e.g. WABC) program   8-9 points
- Lesser quality certification program   1-7 points
- No certification or graduate education   0 points

9. Continuous Development (Coaching) (0-5 points):

If your coach is certified by WABC or comparable organizations, she or he is responsible for regular continuing education to maintain certification. With documented evidence of regular attendance in continuing education courses, etc. to meet certification requirements, assign the coach 5 points. Without documented evidence of maintaining certification, assign no points.

51

10. Ethics Depth (Business) (0-5 points):

Executives are increasingly being evaluated based on their character. Research is starting to track the importance of ethics, integrity and related aspects of character as predictors of success in corporate leadership. As consumers of coaching, these executives expect their coaches to also work with high integrity and ethics.

Executive coaches can join organizations such as the Academy of Management (AOM) and thereby commit to adhering to the AOM's Ethics Code. Coaches with an MBA can subscribe to ethics codes written expressly for them (e.g. *The MBA Oath*). They have opportunities for continuing education in ethics and should document completion of this training for you. Coaches belonging to the AOM or a comparable organization and adhering to their organization's ethics code earn 5 points. Coaches not operating under the AOM or a comparable ethics code earn no points.

11. **Ethics Depth (Psychology) (0-5 points):**

Licensed psychologists are required to understand and adhere to the Ethics Code of the American Psychological Association (APA). Coaches who are licensed psychologists operate under the APA Ethics Code and earn 5 points. Those who are not licensed psychologists or, in the case of psychiatrists, not board certified, and do not operate under the APA or a comparable ethics code earn no points.

12. **Ethics Depth (Coaching) (0-15 points):**

Coaches who are certified by organizations such as WABC and ICF are required to adhere to the organization's ethics code or guidelines. These codes and guidelines are more relevant to the practice of executive coaching than business (e.g. AOM) and psychology (e.g. APA) ethics codes, so they merit 15 points (vs. 5 points each for business and psychological ethics code compliance). Coaches not certified and not operating under a relevant, published ethics code for coaching earn no points.

RECAP—CHAPTER 2

- Executives need to set higher expectations for our coaches. Our executive coaching results could be much better.

- The accuracy of executive coaching choices is limited without key, practical, objective data. The *TEC4* enables consumers—and motivated coaches—to gather the necessary data to make well-informed, savvy decisions.

- There are 4 fundamental areas where a top executive coach should provide strong evidence of depth: Business, Psychology, Coaching and Ethics. The *TEC4* generates clear, comparative information in these areas to help you see the strengths, development opportunities, and other important characteristics of your coaching candidates.

- For 3 of the fundamental areas—Business, Psychology and Coaching—the *TEC4* sets standards and metrics for you to use in evaluating a coach's 1) applied experience, 2) education and training, and 3) continuous development.

- For the 4th fundamental area—Ethics—the *TEC4* sets standards and metrics for you to use in evaluating a coach's degree of compliance with:
  1) an ethics code for businesspeople (e.g. from the Academy of Management)
  2) an ethics code for psychologists (e.g. from the American Psychological Association)
  3) an ethics code for coaches (e.g. from the International Coach Federation).

- All of the *TEC4* standards and metrics are introduced and explained. You can use these pro forma standards and metrics as suggested here, or adapt them for unique situations in your business.

53

- Chapter 4 explains and illustrates adjustments you have the option of making to the *TEC4* standards and metrics to better match your values and priorities.

3

Skirting Landmines

NOW THAT YOU'VE HAD AN INTRODUCTION TO THE *TOP EXECUTIVE COACH 4 (TEC4)* TOOL IN THE PRECEDING CHAPTER, you've seen the outline of how we can assess and score coaches. In this chapter I'll further illustrate how to adjust the *TEC4* with five different types of individuals. I've used fictional characters as prototypes of executive coaches. These prototypes are not based on actual people, but they accurately represent coaching scenarios that are being played out in businesses today.

Let's start with our prototypical coach from Chapter 1, Sam Smith.

Sam Smith

You recall that Sam had 15 high quality years of business experience in different industries. He recently decided to become an executive coach. He had earned a BA in business and economics from a selective and prestigious university in the eastern U.S. Since our initial interview with him and the feedback he heard subsequently, Sam has realized that he needs to align himself with credentialing organizations. He immediately joined the Academy of Management (AOM). He now not only adheres to the AOM Ethics Code, but he keeps copies of it available for prospective clients and he articulates how his work aligns with it in interviews. He also started doing consistent and well-documented work to develop business depth. Finally, Sam started to earn his Worldwide Association of Business Psychologists (WABC) certification. So far he has 88 hours of documented coaching experience. Sam's initial *TEC4* results:

TEC4 Scorecard–Sam Smith

1. Business Depth

• Applied Experience	0-10 points	_7__
• Education & Training	0-10 points	_4__
• Continuous Development	0-5 points	_5__

2. Psychology Depth

• Applied Experience	0-10 points	_0__
• Education & Training	0-10 points	_0__
• Continuous Development	0-5 points	_0__

3. Coaching Depth

• Applied Experience	0-10 points	_1__
• Education & Training	0-10 points	_0__
• Continuous Development	0-5 points	_0__

4. Ethics Depth

• Business Ethics Code	0-5 points	_5__
• Psychology Ethics Code	0-5 points	_0__

• Coaching Ethics Code	0-15 points	_0__
TOTAL	0-100 points	_22__

Sam's *TEC4* score of 22% is in contrast with the energetic sales work he did in talking with you back in Chapter 1. The good news, though, is that his *TEC4* results are now on the table for discussion. You can speak frankly about them with him. Sam can get constructive feedback on his strengths and development needs. He can talk about his background and how he plans to learn and develop. With the *TEC4* providing an objective look at his qualifications, Sam has a chance to ease off the sales pedal and instead build trust with you with directness and openness.

Let's fast-forward 18 months. Prompted by feedback he received from his earlier interview with you and his assessment with the *TEC4*, Sam has wasted no time in building coaching depth. He earned WABC certification. He belongs to the WABC and abides by their ethical guidelines. Based on these guidelines, Sam is also meeting requirements for continuing education in coaching. He increased his total of documented coaching hours from 88 to 300. Now his *TEC4* results reflect his work:

57

TEC4 Scorecard–Sam Smith
(2nd assessment, 18 months later)

1. Business Depth

• Applied Experience	0-10 points	_7__
• Education & Training	0-10 points	_4__
• Continuous Development	0-5 points	_5__

2. Psychology Depth

• Applied Experience	0-10 points	_0__
• Education & Training	0-10 points	_0__
• Continuous Development	0-5 points	_0__

3. Coaching Depth

- Applied Experience   0-10 points   _3__
- Education & Training   0-10 points   _9__
- Continuous Development   0-5 points   _5__

4. Ethics Depth

- Business Ethics Code   0-5 points   _5__
- Psychology Ethics Code   0-5 points   _0__
- Coaching Ethics Code   0-15 points   _15__

TOTAL   0-100 points   _53__

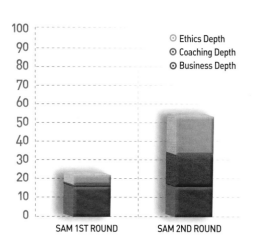

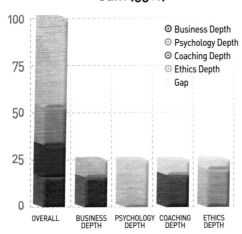

Sam (53%)

At 53%, Sam more than doubled his score and didn't take long doing it. Now he has interesting news for you. He can get back in touch and describe his professional progress and his commitment to consistent future growth. Sam thinks long term and continues building credibility with you that will help build his client base.

Our second prototype has more work experience than Sam.

Ed Executive

Ed is an accomplished industry veteran. He spent 30 years working his way up in financial services and then started out as an executive coach in his mid-50s. Taking advantage of his experience, he targets clients in financial services. He has been coaching now for five years. Earlier in life he earned an MBA at night from a solid, selective program.

Ask Ed how many hours experience he's had in coaching and he'll say that until recently he did not think about becoming certified as an executive coach. He has not been documenting coaching hours over the years. When asked to quantify, however, he claims his total hours to be "well over 1000." A long-time member of the Academy of

Management, Ed complies with their ethics code. Continuing education in business holds little interest for him, though, since he already considers himself an expert in financial services.

Ed plans to apply to a Worldwide Association of Business Coaches (WABC) approved training program in executive coaching. We can see that he is well connected. Many of his coaching clients are former colleagues or clients from his days in financial services. He rightly claims to have considerable industry-specific knowledge and decades of experience at different management levels. Ed's *TEC4* results:

TEC4 Scorecard–Ed Executive

1. Business Depth

• Applied Experience	0-10 points	_9__
• Education & Training	0-10 points	_9__
• Continuous Development	0-5 points	_0__

2. Psychology Depth

• Applied Experience	0-10 points	_0__
• Education & Training	0-10 points	_0__
• Continuous Development	0-5 points	_0__

3. Coaching Depth

• Applied Experience	0-10 points	_0__
• Education & Training	0-10 points	_0__
• Continuous Development	0-5 points	_0__

4. Ethics Depth

• Business Ethics Code	0-5 points	_5__
• Psychology Ethics Code	0-5 points	_0__
• Coaching Ethics Code	0-15 points	_0__
TOTAL	0-100 points	_23__

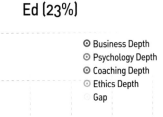

Ed (23%)

Ed has more industry experience than Sam, but his 23% score reveals significant developmental needs Ed must address if he wants to become an outstanding executive coach who is able to communicate his experience, techniques, standards and goals to clients as clearly as possible.

Our third prototypical executive coach, unlike Ed, has no business depth.

Patricia Psychotherapist

Patricia is an excellent clinical psychologist who has been helping her clients work through depression, anxiety, parenting, marital and other important therapeutic issues for 20 years. She earned her PhD in clinical psychology at a top-rated, West Coast university.

She is a licensed psychologist, having passed the American Psychological Association national licensure exam shortly after completing her graduate studies in 1990. As such, she belongs to the American Psychological Association (APA) and is careful to comply with the APA Ethics Code.

Back in her days as a graduate student, Patricia could not

have anticipated how managed mental healthcare (a.k.a. managed care) would someday erode her income and simultaneously weigh her down with administrative work. Now she wants to close her clinical practice.

She hears that executive coaching pays better than psychotherapy and that coaching clients are often healthy and successful people seeking support to continue growing. Patricia thinks ahead. Two years ago, while working as a psychotherapist, she started earning her ICF certification through the College of Executive Coaching program. She has now earned ICF certification, closed her clinical practice, and is in her third year of executive coaching and recently documented her 500th hour. Patricia's *TEC4* results, which would be similar to others' with backgrounds as a counselor, psychiatrist or licensed clinical social worker, look like this:

TEC4 Scorecard–Patricia Psychotherapist

1. Business Depth

• Applied Experience	0-10 points	_0__
• Education & Training	0-10 points	_0__
• Continuous Development	0-5 points	_0__

2. Psychology Depth

• Applied Experience	0-10 points	_10__
• Education & Training	0-10 points	_10__
• Continuous Development	0-5 points	_5__

3. Coaching Depth

• Applied Experience	0-10 points	_4__
• Education & Training	0-10 points	_9__
• Continuous Development	0-5 points	_5__

4. Ethics Depth

• Business Ethics Code	0-5 points	_0__
• Psychology Ethics Code	0-5 points	_5__
• Coaching Ethics Code	0-15 points	_15__

TOTAL   0-100 points   _63__

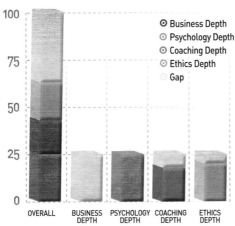

It's impressive that, with just a few years of experience, Patricia is already setting the groundwork to move toward the top of her field. Her 63% score is promising for someone new to executive coaching. Based on her *TEC4* results and feedback, she plans to round out her executive coaching training and qualifications by earning an MBA and joining the Academy of Management (AOM).

Let's look next at how an MBA stacks up on the *TEC4*.

Barry B-School

Barry just celebrated his 31st birthday. His resume lists prestigious universities and employers. He graduated with honors in economics from an Ivy League school. After two years of management consulting for a Big 4 firm, he moved on to a Top 25 Business School. There he did well, ranking in the upper half of his graduating MBA class.

Like many of his classmates, Barry thought about working in investment banking or strategy consulting after graduation. Eventually he accepted an offer from another Big 4 consulting firm than the one where he worked before business school. He also joined the Academy of Management.

Now, in his fifth year of consulting since graduation, Barry spends 80% of every week traveling. He and his wife are about to celebrate the arrival of their first child. It dawns on Barry that his career demands will make it tough to be the involved father he wants to be.

Barry explores other career options. He decides to leave the Big 4 firm and open his own consulting practice, offering strategy consulting and executive coaching. He expects work hours to be more flexible and manageable. He wants to build a book of local clients to minimize out of town travel. He's very social and a good in-person networker, so he starts tapping his database of Ivy alumni.

After 6 months, Barry is primarily consulting and, from time to time, coaching. He has documented 126 coaching hours. His client activity is building slowly. Clients see that Barry has a strong presence, conveying energy and eagerness to help. His *TEC4* results:

TEC4 Scorecard–Barry B-School
1. Business Depth
•	Applied Experience	0-10 points	_4__
•	Education & Training	0-10 points	_10_
•	Continuous Development	0-5 points	_5__

2. Psychology Depth
•	Applied Experience	0-10 points	_0__
•	Education & Training	0-10 points	_0__
•	Continuous Development	0-5 points	_0__

3. Coaching Depth
•	Applied Experience	0-10 points	_0__
•	Education & Training	0-10 points	_0__
•	Continuous Development	0-5 points	_0__

4. Ethics Depth
•	Business Ethics Code	0-5 points	_5__

THE KEY TO FINDING A QUALITY EXECUTIVE COACH

- Psychology Ethics Code   0-5 points   _0__
- Coaching Ethics Code   0-15 points   _0__

     TOTAL   0-100 points   _24_

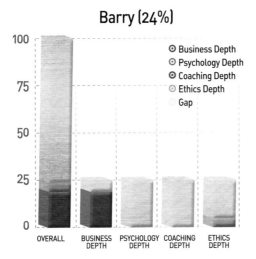

Barry has notable education and achievements to date. His 24% score illustrated in the chart above, however, is in the range of Sam's first score, 22%. Barry has the benefit of *TEC4* feedback, though. To shape himself into a well-regarded, sought-after executive coach, he needs to start addressing his development needs. By creating a targeted plan and getting rolling, he could have the opportunity for decades of effective work.

Susan Sound

Susan is in her early 40's and owes her professional success to hard work, persistence and planning. Her career decisions are well-researched and carefully thought through. She put herself through a fine mid-Atlantic university, majoring in business.

Out of college, she joined a commercial real estate firm and, in keeping with her intelligence and work ethic, did well. Along the way, she took advantage of her firm's policy of reimbursing MBA educational expenses. She completed her business school degree back at her alma mater.

After 15 years at the real estate firm, Susan felt she had learned as much as possible. She also noticed one of her motivations getting stronger—to help people grow and develop. Eventually, with encouragement and guidance from friends, colleagues and mentors, she decided to become an executive coach.

Unlike many new coaches, Susan started her career transition by carefully studying the executive coaching industry. She concluded that certification would improve her competitive position. Consequently, she started working on her coaching certification several months before announcing her departure from the real estate firm. The certification work helped her confirm that, based on her talents and goals, she was moving on the right professional path.

Two years after launching her coaching career, Susan earned certification by the International Association of Coaches (IAC). She then joined both the IAC and the Academy of Management (AOM). She is complying with continuing education and ethical requirements of these organizations, and with seven years of coaching behind her, her documented coaching hours number 1,000.

Thinking ahead further, Susan enrolled in a Master of Science (MS) program in industrial-organizational psychology at a nearby university. After four years of evening classes, she is about to graduate. She joins the American Psychological Association as a student at a discounted rate. Susan's *TEC4* results:

TEC4 Scorecard–Susan Sound
1. Business Depth
• Applied Experience	0-10 points	_7__
• Education & Training	0-10 points	_7__
• Continuous Development	0-5 points	_5__

2. Psychology Depth
• Applied Experience	0-10 points	_0__
• Education & Training	0-10 points	_4__
• Continuous Development	0-5 points	_5__

3. Coaching Depth
• Applied Experience	0-10 points	_6__
• Education & Training	0-10 points	_9__
• Continuous Development	0-5 points	_5__

4. Ethics Depth
• Business Ethics Code	0-5 points	_5__
• Psychology Ethics Code	0-5 points	_5__
• Coaching Ethics Code	0-15 points	_15__
TOTAL	0-100 points	_73__

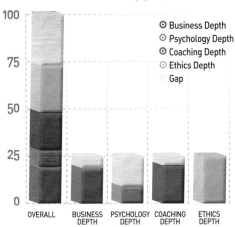

Susan (73%)

We can predict that, now in her mid-40s, Susan has at least another 25 years of executive coaching in front of her. With her work ethic and planning skills, it's logical to assume she'll continue her professional development. Her already acceptable score, 73%, will probably rise.

Susan is tracking toward the upper tier of her field. She will be delivering fine results to her clients consistently. In addition, whenever prospective clients or buyers want to compare Susan with other coaches, particularly using the *TEC4*, she will be confident in her professional standing and will encourage these comparisons.

Scoring Recap

Our five prototypes had these *TEC4* scores:

- Sam Smith (1ˢᵗ assessment)   22%
- Sam Smith (2ⁿᵈ assessment)   53%
- Ed Executive   23%
- Patricia Psychotherapist   63%
- Barry B-School   24%
- Susan Sound   73%

68

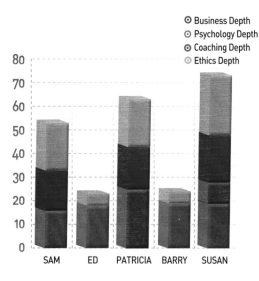

As a consumer of executive coaching, you'll encounter folks like Sam, Ed, Patricia, Barry and Susan—as well as other prototypes—often. Each will present differently, accentuating strengths and diverting your attention from their gaps. Fortunately the *TEC4* tool cuts through this maneuvering to generate meaningful, comparative information for us. It helps guide our questions and discussions with prospective executive coaches and provides the unvarnished data needed to make an objective decision. The resulting benefit is a thorough, clear, apples-to-apples executive coaching selection process.

The *TEC4* Approach vs. Others

Let's take a moment to see how thoroughly Sam, Ed, Patricia, Barry and Susan would be screened with executive coaching selection approaches recommended by others. Let's assume for the moment that Susan, with a 73% *TEC4* score, is the only candidate coach with acceptable results to make our first cut.

Recently a human resources magazine offered these helpful tips for picking an executive coach:

69

- *Get referrals to good potential coaches from your network of people you trust.*
- *Interview candidate coaches to find out about how they work and what level of executive they work with best.*
- *Work to create a group of top quality coaches from which you can match the 'best-fitting coach' to the coachee.*
- *Look for coaches with flexible approaches who are not limited to a certain methodology or way of working.*
- *Be certain the coach follows an ethical coaching code and generates a coaching contract with specific and measurable goals.*
- *Look for an executive coach with an enthusiastic, positive attitude that inspires confidence, and who is well-qualified in coaching techniques and models.*
- *After selecting a short-list of candidates, check out their references.*

- *Ask each coaching candidate to meet with the coachee to spotlight their coaching skills—picking an issue to discuss for 10 minutes—to demonstrate how well the two people might work together.*
- *To help match your coachee with the right coach, explore with your candidate coaches 1) the client issues they have worked on and 2) their areas of strengths and weaknesses.*
- *Pay special attention to the person to be coached—so he or she has a key role in the selection and in particular is comfortable with the 'chemistry' with the selected coach.*

Let's go through this list and see how each point compares with what the *TEC4* offers us.

- *Get referrals to good potential coaches from your network of people you trust.*

These referrals can be helpful assuming that 1) people you trust have themselves first carefully evaluated the executive coaches they now consider "good" and 2) people you trust have a clear ranking of their executive coaches' overall quality and can explain their process for ranking the coaches. You'll need to know what "good" means and in comparison to what, exactly. Sam, Ed, Patricia, Barry and Susan could all point us to well-meaning and positive references.

- *Interview candidate coaches to find out about how they work and what level of executive they work with best.*

It's always helpful to interview candidates and to explore how they work and what level of executives they work with best. These are two of many topics to dig into in meeting with executive coaches. Sam, Ed, Patricia, Barry and Susan would all respond with solid answers to both topics. But then how have you differentiated the five of them?

- *Work to create a group of top quality coaches from which you can match the 'best-fitting coach' to the coachee.*

It's an excellent goal to have a stable of fine executive coaches to pick from. But how will you specifically evaluate and identify the right coaches to have in your stable? Is there any clear reason why Sam, Ed, Patricia, Barry or Susan would not belong in the stable?

- *Look for coaches with flexible approaches who are not limited to a certain methodology or way of working.*

Without a specific and proven methodology or process for coaching executives, a candidate might still be able to talk about various ways of working while emphasizing his or her flexibility based on your needs. All five of our prototypical executive coaches could prep themselves to do well in that discussion.

- *Be certain the coach follows an ethical coaching code and generates a coaching contract with specific and measurable goals*

This tip has value in that it provides no wiggle room for candidates who are not able to substantiate their membership in a coaching organization and to produce a copy of that organization's code of ethics. Sam (in his second evaluation), Patricia and Susan would be fine here. Ed and Barry would not.

- *Look for an executive coach with an enthusiastic, positive attitude that inspires confidence, and who is well-qualified in coaching techniques and models.*

Any of our prototypical executive coaches can convey enthusiasm and confidence in an interview. How specifically could we verify how "well-qualified" our coaches are in coaching techniques and models, though? Any of the five can Google "coaching models and techniques" and become conversant, right? If we insisted on formal training and credentialing in coaching, Sam (in his second evaluation), Patricia and Susan would pass and, again, Ed and Barry would not.

- *After selecting a short-list of candidates, check out their references.*

I have two questions here. First, how exactly do you narrow the field down to the short list? Steps for doing that are not defined. Second, as we noted for the first tip of this section, how do you know how reliable and discriminating the references are before you "check them out?" All five prototypes jump easily through this hoop, correct?

- *Ask each coaching candidate to meet with the coachee to spotlight their coaching skills—picking an issue to discuss for 10 minutes—to demonstrate how well the two people might work together.*

The value of a face-to-face meeting is high, so this tip is worthwhile. A complimentary coaching session of 60—90 minutes (not 10) is much more revealing however. How likely is it that any of our prototypical executive coaches would struggle to show well for just 10 minutes?

- *To help match your coachee with the right coach, explore with your candidate coaches 1) the client issues they have worked on and 2) their areas of strengths and weaknesses.*

It doesn't take a cynic to realize that any coach could read up on typical client issues and carry on that conversation as long as that coach didn't have to substantiate his or her work with clients by citing them as specific examples. Similarly, coaches you evaluate are free to comment on their perceptions of their own strengths and weaknesses, but without data like the *TEC4* results, how do you substantiate their comments? With the experience they have, none of the five prototypes would find this exploration particularly challenging, and the results of a candidate driven discussion would not provide you with much useful information.

- *Pay special attention to the person to be coached—so he or she has a key role in the selection and in particular is comfortable with the 'chemistry' with the selected coach.*

This makes good sense. We assume the coachee has most of the input into the coaching selection; his or her comfort with the chemistry with a candidate coach is important. However, other than a feel for the chemistry with a coach, what exactly are you to rely on to differentiate among coaches and pick the strongest one? Coaches of almost any quality can encourage good chemistry and a favorable first impression.

Let's look at a few more screening questions recommended in the executive coaching literature. These are questions for you to ask your candidate.

- *What training in coaching have you received?*
- *Have you coached individuals in my industry?*
- *How will you assess my current skills and how will you measure improvement?*

How do each of these questions compare with what can be learned with the *TEC4*?

- *What training in coaching have you received?*

Let's think back to Sam's answers in Chapter 1. Remember how he suggested that he had learned a lot about executive coaching from his experience as an executive? He also could have claimed to have learned a lot from other executives and even other executive coaches he knew. He never confirmed any formal training in coaching. Sam later got formal training, as did Patricia and Susan. If Ed and Barry couldn't talk their way around this question, perhaps the gaps in their expertise would be exposed and you could screen them out.

- *Have you coached individuals in my industry?*

If the candidate coach has industry-specific experience, it may be a positive. However, a coach's experience in the same specific business function or industry as the client is a double-edged sword. Too much familiarity can handicap the coach, leading to nuts-and-bolts discussions and shop talk when the coach's real job is to help the client find ways to manage and lead better so the client is most successful in solving his or her own business problems.

- *How will you assess my current skills and how will you measure improvement?*

If you expect to hear specifics about topics such as use of the Watson-Glaser Critical Thinking Appraisal from the candidate coach, then this question could effectively screen out Sam, Ed, Barry and possibly Susan. However, if you're content with vague but reassuring answers like "I know from experience which approaches work best in evaluating my clients' strengths and development needs," then any of our five prototypes could pass this screen.

Let's summarize the preceding comments:

1. The literature offers us many suggestions for evaluating

executive coaches.

2. Practically all these suggestions help as we're starting to learn about a candidate coach.

3. Many of the suggestions help us form a first impression of a candidate.

4. Some suggestions encourage us to learn more, digging deeper with the candidate.

5. Often these suggestions could be more pointed and specific to help us generate objective and subjective information sufficient to actually compare and rank executive coaches—so we can be most effective in screening candidates and winding up with the best possible choice.

RECAP–CHAPTER 3

- The *TEC4* tool that was first described in Chapter 2 is explained further. We illustrate how easy it is to use by working through and obtaining *TEC4* scores (0-100%) for 5 prototypical executive coaches that consumers and other coaches often encounter in the marketplace.

- Prototype #1: Sam Smith is an executive with 15 years of work experience. Sam scores poorly (22%) in his first *TEC4* assessment. Eighteen months later, after learning about his strengths and development areas in the first assessment, Sam has made excellent use of his learning. He addresses a number of development opportunities. This time, he scores better (53%) on the *TEC4*.

- Prototype #2: Ed Executive is a veteran executive with 30 years of work experience. While he has twice the work experience of Sam, his *TEC4* score is similarly poor (23%). To be the most successful and marketable coach possible Ed has lots of development work ahead.

- Prototype #3: Patricia Psychologist is clinical psychologist with 20 years of experience in working with her psychotherapy clients. After deciding to become an executive coach, she plans ahead and wastes little time getting as much education and training as possible. For example, she earns her coaching certification before stopping her psychotherapy work. Her *TEC4* score is 63% and is expected to keep rising.

- Prototype #4: Barry B-School is in his early 30s, with an MBA from a prestigious top 25 program. Barry spends 5 years working for a Big 4 consultancy after business school. He then decides to be an independent consultant offering strategy consulting and executive coaching. His poor *TEC4* score, 24%, gives Barry clear and practical feedback on how to chart his career development.

- Prototype #5: Susan Sound has 15 years of experience working for a real estate firm. A few years ago she earned her MBA at night while working. She is proactive and forward-thinking, and after just 2 years in executive coaching she has a 73% *TEC4* score. We can predict success for her in this new career.

- The executive coaching literature includes suggestions, check-lists and other tips for selecting an executive coach. Almost all this information is valuable. It is often useful in alerting us to look for and ask about certain qualities in the candidate coach. However, to make the best-informed choice, we would benefit from considerably more detailed and objective data to screen candidates thoroughly and accurately.

Flexing
Accurately

Building Value

TEC4 SCORES HELP YOU RANK AND IDEN-TIFY QUALITY IN EXECUTIVE COACHES IN STAGE 1 OF THE SELECTION PROCESS.

By making a confident and well-informed first cut of candidates, you save time and money and immediately reduce your chance of a bad selection.

In the previous chapter, we used the *TEC4* to score five prototypical executive coaches. We used the recommended—or pro forma—approach to awarding points in each of the four *TEC4* categories: Business Depth, Psychology Depth, Coaching Depth and Ethics Depth.

In Stage 1 we do our initial data gathering and screening of coaches via, for example, phone, email, Skype, business networks (e.g. LinkedIn www.linkedin.com) or face to face meetings. We drill down and are guided by the *TEC4* to clarify detailed information, more precisely compare and contrast candidate coaches and make a knowledgeable first cut.

In this chapter I'll give three examples of adjusting the pro forma *TEC4* scoring approach we first used. While many people prefer the universality of the first, standard approach, others want to use *TEC4*'s flexibility and versatility to more closely match their values and needs.

You'll see that the *TEC4* flexes to incorporate our individual adjustments, providing the same consistent, comparable and useful information we generate when using the *TEC4* on the standard basis.

78

Three Scenarios

For any of the 12 items of the *TEC4—Continuous Development (Coaching)*, for example—point ranges can be changed. What follows are examples of adjusted point ranges for three different scenarios.

Scenario #1: Decreasing the Value of Applied Experience

Let's suppose that you (the consumer) grew up in a family that placed high value on formal education and training, and that your own views reflect this. Perhaps with the *TEC4* you want to put more emphasis on education and training. Since you have a total of 25 points in each of the four fundamental areas (Business Depth, Psychology Depth, Coaching Depth, Ethics Depth), you 1) *increase points allocated to education and training, and continuous development* and 2) *decrease points allocated to applied experience*. Point ranges of the 12 items of the *TEC4* are changeable, for example, as follows:

1. Applied Experience (Business):
   cut range from 0-10 to 0-5 points
2. Education & Training (Business):
   raise range from 0-10 to 0-14 points
3. Continuous Development (Business):
   raise range from 0-5 to 0-6 points

4. Applied Experience (Psychology) :
   cut range from 0-10 to 0-5 points
5. Education & Training (Psychology):
   raise range from 0-10 to 0-14 points
6. Continuous Development (Psychology):
   raise range from 0-5 to 0-6 points

7. Applied Experience (Coaching):
   cut range from 0-10 to 0-5 points
8. Education & Training (Coaching):
   raise range from 0-10 to 0-14 points
9. Continuous Development (Coaching):
   raise range from 0-5 to 0-6 points

10. Business Ethics Code: **unchanged:** 0-5 points
11. Psychology Ethics Code: **unchanged:** 0-5 points
12. Coaching Ethics Code: **unchanged:** 0-15 points

The *TEC4* scorecard changes to look this way:

TEC4 Scorecard - Scenario #1
(decreasing the value of Applied Experience)

1. Business Depth

• Applied Experience	0-5 points	____
• Education & Training	0-14 points	____
• Continuous Development	0-6 points	____

2. Psychology Depth
- Applied Experience   0-5 points   ____
- Education & Training   0-14 points   ____
- Continuous Development   0-6 points   ____

3. Coaching Depth
- Applied Experience   0-5 points   ____
- Education & Training   0-14 points   ____
- Continuous Development   0-6 points   ____

4. Ethics Depth
- Business Ethics Code   0-5 points   ____
- Psychology Ethics Code   0-5 points   ____
- Coaching Ethics Code   0-15 points   ____

            TOTAL   0-100 points   ____

Next, we change scoring guides for the 12 *TEC4* items. The following example is for *Applied Experience (Business),* the first item under the category Business Depth. Recall that we just cut the total point range for this item from 0-10 to 0-5. Consequently, we change the scoring guide for this item as follows:

- 20+ yrs. of high quality experience
    cut from 10 points to 5 points
- 20+ yrs. of good quality experience
    cut from 8-9 points to 4 points
- 11-19 yrs. of high quality experience
    cut from 6-7 points to 3-4 points
- 11-19 yrs. of good quality experience
    cut from 5 points to 3 points
- 5-10 yrs. of high quality experience
    cut from 4 points to 2-3 points
- 5-10 yrs. of good quality experience
    cut from 3 points to 2 points

- 1-4 yrs. of high quality experience
  cut from 2 points to 1 point
- 1-4 yrs. of good quality experience
  cut from 1 point to 0 points

Similarly, we change scoring guides for the other items including *Education & Training (Business), Continuous Development (Business), Education & Training (Psychology), Applied Experience (Psychology), Continuous Development (Psychology), Education & Training (Coaching), Applied Experience (Coaching) and Continuous Development (Coaching).*

We would not adjust scoring guides for the last 3 items of the *TEC4: Business Ethics Code, Psychology Ethics Code,* and *Coaching Ethics Code.* These items do not change.

In this first scenario, our characters Sam, Ed, Patricia, Barry and Susan generate the following scores. In the first column you'll see their scores from the pro forma *TEC4*, the second shows how they rank when we put less value on *Applied Experience.*

	1.	2.
Sam Smith (2nd assessment)	53	55
Ed Executive	23	20
Patricia Psychotherapist	63	65
Barry B-School	24	22
Susan Sound	73	82

Scenario #2: Decreasing the Value of Education & Training, Continuous Development

Here's a second example. Let's suppose this time you (the consumer) grew up in a family of people who succeeded mostly from on—the—job training and hands on work experience. Formal education and training played less of a role; you were taught that they made little difference in happiness, success, etc. So in considering the *TEC4* you elect to 1) *increase points allocated for Applied Experience* and 2) *decrease points allocated for Education & Training* and *Continuous Development.*

As in Scenario #1, we change scoring guides of *TEC4* items (example below) while keeping the total number of points at 25 in each of the 4 categories (Business Depth, Psychology Depth, Coaching Depth and Ethics Depth):

1. Applied Experience (Business):
   raise range from 0-10 to 0-18 points
2. Education & Training (Business):
   cut range from 0-10 to 0-5 points
3. Continuous Development (Business):
   cut range from 0-5 to 0-2 points

4. Applied Experience (Psychology):
   raise range from 0-10 to 0-18 points
5. Education & Training (Psychology):
   cut range from 0-10 to 0-5 points
6. Continuous Development (Psychology):
   cut range from 0-5 to 0-2 points

7. Applied Experience (Coaching):
   raise range from 0-10 to 0-18 points
8. Education & Training (Coaching):
   cut range from 0-10 to 0-5 points
9. Continuous Development (Coaching):
   cut range from 0-5 to 0-2 points

10. Business Ethics Code: **unchanged:** 0-5 points
11. Psychology Ethics Code: **unchanged:** 0-5 points
12. Coaching Ethics Code: **unchanged:** 0-15 points

The *TEC4* scorecard changes to look this way:

TEC4 Scorecard – Scenario #2 (decreasing the Value of Education & Training, & Continuous Development)

1. Business Depth

• Applied Experience	0-18 points	____
• Education & Training	0-5 points	____
• Continuous Development	0-2 points	____

2. Psychology Depth

• Applied Experience	0-18 points	____
• Education & Training	0-5 points	____
• Continuous Development	0-2 points	____

3. Coaching Depth

• Applied Experience	0-18 points	____
• Education & Training	0-5 points	____
• Continuous Development	0-2 points	____

4. Ethics Depth

• Business Ethics Code	0-5 points	____
• Psychology Ethics Code	0-5 points	____
• Coaching Ethics Code	0-15 points	____
TOTAL	0-100 points	____

83

Then, as we did in Scenario #1, we change scoring guides for the *TEC4* items. Let's again use *Applied Experience (Business)* as an example. Remember that we just changed the range of points for this item from 0-10 to 0-18. So we also change the scoring guide for this item as follows:

- 20+ yrs. of high quality experience
  raise from 10 points to 18 points
- 20+ yrs. of good quality experience
  raise from 8-9 points to 16-17 points

- 11-19 yrs. of high quality experience
  raise from 6-7 points to 13-15 points
- 11-19 yrs. of good quality experience
  raise from 5 points to 11-12 points
- 5-10 yrs. of high quality experience
  raise from 4 points to 8-10 points
- 5-10 yrs. of good quality experience
  raise from 3 points to 5-7 points
- 1-4 yrs. of high quality experience
  raise from 2 points to 3-4 points
- 1-4 yrs. of good quality experience
  raise from 1 point to 2 points

We also change scoring guides for other items including *Education & Training (Business), Continuous Development (Business), Education & Training (Psychology), Applied Experience (Psychology), Continuous Development (Psychology), Education & Training (Coaching), Applied Experience (Coaching)* and *Continuous Development (Coaching).*

Decreasing the value of *Education & Training* and *Continuous Development* does not affect scoring guides for the last three *TEC4* items, *Business Ethics Code, Psychology Ethics Code,* and *Coaching Ethics Code.* These items remain the same.

Sam, Ed, Patricia, Barry and Susan's scores appear below. Column 1 is our pro forma assessment, column 2 are scores when we decrease the value of *Applied Experience,* and column 3 shows results when we decrease the value of *Training and Education,* and of *Continuous Development.*

	1.	2.	3.
Sam Smith (2nd assessment)	53	55	51
Edward Executive	22	20	26
Patricia Psychotherapist	63	65	54

Barry B-School	24	22	22
Susan Sound	73	82	64

Scenario #3: Decreasing the Value of Business and Psychology Ethics Codes

In this third example, you (the consumer) take the position that since you are evaluating executive coaches, the only ethics codes that matter are those designed specifically for coaching. Ethics codes for business (e.g. Academy of Management) and psychology (e.g. American Psychological Association), while setting admirable and high standards, are less important to you than, for instance, ethics codes from the Worldwide Association of Business Coaches (WABC) or the International Coach Federation (ICF).

Here, we adjust scoring guides for three *TEC4* items *(Business Ethics Code, Psychology Ethics Code,* and *Coaching Ethics Code)* making up the fourth fundamental category, *Ethics Depth.* The other nine items making up the first three fundamental categories *(Business Depth, Psychology Depth and Coaching Depth)* are not changed since they do not affect ethical standards.

So our *TEC4* scoring guides changes to:

1. Applied Experience (Business):
    unchanged: 0-10 points
2. Education & Training (Business):
    unchanged: 0-10 points
3. Continuous Development (Business):
    unchanged: 0-5 points

4. Applied Experience (Psychology):
    unchanged: 0-10 points
5. Education & Training (Psychology):
    unchanged: 0-10 points
6. Continuous Development (Psychology):
    unchanged: 0-5 points

7. Applied Experience (Coaching):
   unchanged: 0-10 points
8. Education & Training (Coaching):
   unchanged: 0-10 points
9. Continuous Development (Coaching):
   unchanged: 0-5 points

10. Business Ethics Code: **cut** from 0-5 points to 0 points
11. Psychology Ethics Code: **cut** from 0-5 points to 0 points
12. Coaching Ethics Code: **raise** from 0-15 to 0-25 points

The *TEC4* scorecard now looks this way:

TEC4 Scorecard - Scenario #3 (decreasing the value of Business and Psychology Ethics Codes)

1. Business Depth
• Applied Experience	0-10 points	____
• Education & Training	0-10 points	____
• Continuous Development	0-5 points	____

2. Psychology Depth
• Applied Experience	0-10 points	____
• Education & Training	0-10 points	____
• Continuous Development	0-5 points	____

3. Coaching Depth
• Applied Experience	0-10 points	____
• Education & Training	0-10 points	____
• Continuous Development	0-5 points	____

4. Ethics Depth
• Business Ethics Code	0 points	____
• Psychology Ethics Code	0 points	____
• Coaching Ethics Code	0-25 points	____
TOTAL	0-100 points	____

Scoring for the item *Coaching Ethics Code* in this example is simple. WABC, IAC, ICF or another comparable coaching certification yardstick earns 25 points. Points are not awarded for adhering to either a *Business Ethics Code* or a *Psychology Ethics Code*.

Scoring Recap and Consistency

We used the *TEC4* to score Sam, Ed, Patricia, Barry and Susan in this third scenario (results listed in column four below). Overall, their four sets of *TEC4* scores are:

Sam Smith (2nd assessment)	53	55	51	58
Ed Executive	22	20	26	17
Patricia Psychotherapist	63	65	54	68
Barry B-School	24	22	22	19
Susan Sound	73	82	64	73

We naturally think our own circumstances are unique, so of course we wonder: is the standard, pro forma version of a tool like the *TEC4* sensitive enough to capture and reflect our situation and values? Do we get comparable value from the *TEC4* in evaluating coaches when 1) we use the standard, pro forma version and 2) we make adjustments to the standard, pro forma version?

The answer to both of these questions is yes.

Looking at the *TEC4* scores above, we notice that there is little variation in the scores and rankings of our five prototypes. Results from the standard scenario and the other three adjusted scenarios are consistent, illustrating the versatility and value of the *TEC4* regardless of how we apply it.

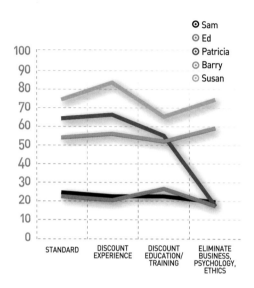

So overall we took advantage of *TEC4* flexibility and consistency to generate three additional sets of useful scores (in the chart above) by adjusting scoring guides for each of the 12 *TEC4* items (e.g. *Education & Training (Psychology)*) with three different assumptions (e.g. decreasing the value of *Education and Training*, and *Continuous Development*).

The Final Step

To summarize, the *TEC4* helps us make informed, data-oriented decisions in our initial, Stage 1 scan or first cut of executive coaches under consideration. It provides us with this decision-making support whether we use the standard (recommended) scoring approach introduced in Chapter 3 or adjusted approaches such as those three illustrated in this chapter.

Stage 1 in the selection process uses relatively objective data: specific findings about depth and qualifications in business, psychology, coaching and ethics. In the next chapter, we'll look at Stage 2, the final step in the selection process, when additional secondary characteristics are revealed to help us narrow down the field and find the executive coach with the strongest experience and expertise to make a difference in our company.

How Our Five Prototypes Fared

You may be thinking about how Sam, Ed, Patricia, Barry and Susan are doing in our evaluation so far. The answer of course depends on our assumptions in evaluating their *TEC4* information.

Let's assume that we take a relatively strict (vs. lax) view of *TEC4* scores. I typically suggest this approach because it increases both efficiency and effectiveness in choosing a coach. If for example we think of A level scores in the 90–100% range, B level scores in the 80–89% range, and C level scores in the 70–79% range, it makes sense to set our cut-off point at 70% or higher.

On this basis, we can move Susan (73%) on to Stage 2 of our evaluation. She should be scheduled as soon as possible for the Stage 2 interview (to be discussed in the next chapter) for two reasons. First, if she does well in the Stage 2 interview, we have our best choice and she can start working with our coachee.

Second, if for some reason we are uncomfortable or concerned about Susan after the Stage 2 interview, we'll be faced with decisions including 1) are we willing to compromise our 70% minimum to invite Patricia (63%) into Stage 2, and 2) if we don't invite Patricia, are we willing to take more time to identify additional new candidate coaches (besides the original five) to evaluate—starting again at Stage 1? Time permitting, it makes a lot of sense to bring in new candidates.

Let's assume for discussion purposes, though, that we're really pressed for time. Let's also assume we were uncomfortable with Susan during her Stage 2 interview, we compromised and invited Patricia into Stage 2, we were happy with Patricia at the end of her Stage 2 interview, and we hired Patricia.

As ethical and responsible executives, what else would we

consider doing?

It would help everyone involved in the process if we invited the coaches not selected (Susan, Sam, Ed and Barry) to follow up meetings to provide 1) clear, constructive feedback about their strengths and development needs and 2) suggestions for building on their strengths and addressing their development needs. We'd also have a chance to hear feedback from these four candidates that might help us refine our evaluation process.

RECAP – CHAPTER 4

- Armed with *TEC4* scores, you (the consumer) have considerable and more objective information with which to identify quality and to rank candidate coaches.

- You may choose to tailor *TEC4* standards and metrics to align more closely with your priorities and values or your specific situation.

- Three hypothetical scenarios are offered to illustrate versatility, consistency and flexibility in the *TEC4*.

- Scenario #1: The value system you (the consumer) developed in growing up gives you the following lens in considering how to use the *TEC4*: formal education and training is more meaningful and valuable to you in evaluating coaches, and applied experience is not particularly important. We adjust the *TEC4* accordingly and then use it to generate scores for our five prototypical executive coaches.

- Scenario #2: The reverse of Scenario #1 – applied experience is most important to you in evaluating coaches, and formal education and training is less important. We adjust the *TEC4* accordingly to generate scores for our five prototypical executive coaches.

- Scenario #3: A variation of Scenarios #1 and #2. Here, based on years of professional experience, you decide that coaching ethics codes are most important and that business ethics codes and psychology ethics codes have no value. Again, we adjust the *TEC4* and score our five prototypical executive coaches.

- *TEC4* results for our prototypes are comparable under the standard, pro forma scenario and in each of the three adjusted scenarios. The prototypes are essentially ranked the same each time, for example.

91

- The *TEC4* is consistent and versatile, providing us with strong decision-making support and information whether we use the standard scoring approach or a customized (adjusted) approach.

Final Cuts

SELECTING A TOP QUALITY EXECUTIVE COACH IS SIMILAR TO PICKING THE TOP CANDIDATE FOR ANY JOB AND INCLUDES TWO STEPS. First, we use the *TEC4* to evaluate coaching candidates and then to trim our list based on the four fundamentals (Business Depth, Psychology Depth, Coaching Depth and Ethics Depth) discussed previously.

Stage 1 in the selection process—gathering information for *TEC4* scoring—can be conducted via, for example, phone, email, Skype, social networks (e.g. LinkedIn *www.linkedin.com*) or face to face meetings. We're guided by the *TEC4* to make a well-informed first cut.

Stage 2 in the selection process is to interview the remaining candidate(s) in person, if at all possible. Face-to-face meetings are important, and we'll go into that more. For the moment, keep the following in mind as you meet with the candidate coaches who survived your first cut.

How to Value Important Characteristics

In Chapter 2 we made a list of just a few of hundreds of useful characteristics and skills executive coaches may have that are hard for us to quantify and measure:

> ....*assertiveness, openness, flexibility, goal orientation, partnering, continuous learning, integrity, facilitating development, promoting change, maturity, self-confidence, positivity, energy, interpersonal sensitivity, multicultural awareness, contracting, development planning, influencing, aligning, allying, transitioning, inquiring, trustworthiness, approachability, political savvy, curiosity, self-awareness, delegation, confrontation, giving feedback, goal-setting, training, reinforcement, active listening, time management, meeting management, problem-solving, conflict resolution…and on and on.*

We could spend a lot of time adding to this list. The key question, though, is this: Would doing so *clarify* or *confuse* the choice of the best coach? As it currently stands, the list is endless, already more confusing than clarifying.

More words do not equal more helpful. Consumers benefit most from clear guidance about which particular criteria are most important and from ways to explore these most important criteria with coaching candidates. You don't need more words, you need practical information about the relative value of each descriptive word.

There is one other variable to pay attention to. Thinking back to the confusing marketing messages we get from coaches, it is clear that each characteristic or skill on our list is essentially another chance for coaching candidates to try to justify why he or she is the top candidate. However, if consumers—and not the coach—control the agenda of the Stage 2 interview and choose topics to explore with the coach, there is less chance of being pitched to by the candidate coach and losing control of the interview.

The Face-to-Face Meeting

In this second stage of selection, I recommend the following approach to sorting through intangible but important characteristics. I want to make the vague and unwieldy more structured and useful for you. Consequently, below are five topics to talk through with the coaches who survive Stage 1 in your selection.

Meet with each candidate for at least 90 minutes. Let each candidate know that he or she is one of a number of candidates and that this face-to-face meeting is important in your process of learning more. During the interview and afterwards, write down your reactions—whatever you hear, see, think and feel.

For each of the five topics for exploration with a potential coach, there are sample questions. The purpose of these questions is to generate information, the *content* of your interview.

Equally important, however, is the *context* of your interview. As the coaching candidate responds to your questions, pay attention to your feelings and gut reactions. How is the coach coming across? You can take a moment to consider why you feel, for example, comfortable, suspicious, relaxed, calm, anxious, tense, confused, misunderstood or trusting, to name just a few potential reactions.

95

Five Areas to Explore

For several decades, psychiatrists, psychologists, counselors and other professionals have examined various human dimensions to learn about their clients and patients. Five of these key dimensions are:

- Intellectual /Thinking Abilities (e.g. problem solving)

- Emotional Characteristics (e.g. values, motivation, feelings)
- Interpersonal Preferences (e.g. impact on others)
- Insight (e.g. self-awareness, the ability to read situations involving others)
- Leadership/Work Styles (e.g. control needs, delegation, participative vs. demanding)

There is nothing mystical or magical about these five areas. They have been widely used for decades to help us understand more about the person sitting across the table. Let's apply them to the executive coach interview. Below in Sections 1 through 4 are questions for you to ask the coach, and in Section 5 are questions for you to consider. After everything is answered, we'll process what you've discovered.

Ask each candidate the following, and notice if the coach responds with a lot of buzz words and jargon or explains ideas fully, crisply and clearly.

1. Intellectual / Problem-solving Abilities

- How do you analyze issues, reach solutions and solve problems? Are you more logical than intuitive, or vice-versa? Why?
- Explain your methods and why they are effective. Do you use any particular coaching methods? Why? (Take note of how clearly the candidate answers.)
- What level(s) of executives (e.g. entry level managers, C-level leaders) do you brainstorm or problem-solve with? Examples?
- What is your knowledge and experience level in my industry?
- Tell me how you've experienced challenges and issues varying with clients in different organizational roles at different levels?
- How do you apply your expertise in business, psychology,

coaching and ethics in working with clients? Specific examples?
- How flexible are you as a thinker and problem solver? How open are you to others' ideas? Examples?
- How do you learn about new concepts or findings in your field? Would you give me some examples?
- How do you work to add to your knowledge of, for example, business, psychology, coaching and ethics?

After listening for a while to the coach, for example, how are you reacting to his or her comments? Bored, spellbound, lost? Do you feel the coach is making logical, realistic comments? Why or why not?

2. Emotional Characteristics
- What are you passionate about?
- What drives you? What are your priorities?
- How resilient and persistent are you in the face of obstacles to goals? Examples?
- How well do you tolerate stress? Examples?
- How direct and transparent are you with feelings and thoughts?
- What makes you happy? Frustrated? Distracted? Excited?
- What's your motivation as a coach? Is it to build your client's skills and success or to become a necessary support? Why?
- What are you most proud of? Why?

97

Take careful note of how the coach reacts to your asking all these questions. What could his or her demeanor be saying? Without artificial hype, how enthusiastic, confident and energizing is the coach to be around? Do you sense the coach is direct and truthful or is saying what he thinks you want to hear? Does the coach seem secure? How much time and energy does she spend talking about herself versus learning about you and what's important to you?

3. Insight

- How do you view yourself? (In your opinion, how close is this coach's view to what you are seeing? Why?)
- How well do you understand your own biases? How do you steer around them in working with clients? Examples?
- What are important points or events in life that contributed significantly to your development? How? Why?
- Who do you look up to or aspire to be as an exceptional, best-in-class executive coach? Why?
- What would people who know you well say are your top 3-5 strengths? Bottom 3-5 weaknesses? Why?
- How helpful or challenging would your mix of strengths and weaknesses be for me as your client?
- Can you provide a fresh perspective on my situation and goals? Why?
- How do you learn about the people around you? How do you adjust to them? Examples?
- What have been the most important professional and personal experiences for you? Why?
- If you waved a magic wand and became perfect, what specifically would change about you? Why?
- What was your ideal of excellent coaching when you began work as a coach? How (if at all) has this ideal changed over the years? Why?

4. Leadership / Work Style

- What's your style working with clients? Motivating? Open? Frank? Organized? Informal? Demanding? Authoritative? Global or linear?

- What is your role in empowering and developing others?
- If 10 means efficient micromanager and 0 means excellent delegator, what number are you? Why?
- Are you a glass half full or half empty person? Why?
- How bottom-line and decisive are you? How often do you make suggestions and expect the client to decide? Examples?
- What are your ethical responsibilities to your clients?
- What are your thoughts on how adults learn and grow? How do you encourage and facilitate adult growth and behavior change?
- How do you plan work and manage the relationship with the client?
- How practical vs. theoretical or conceptual are you? How well do you see your approach fitting my situation? Why?
- What are your biggest challenges in working with clients?
- Do you feel that you are more respected or appreciated by your clients?
- Is your work-style based more on 'steak' (e.g. substantive knowledge and skill) or 'sizzle' (e.g. pep-talks, cheerleading)? Why?
- If 10 means you absolutely loving your work and 0 means you do it out of a sense of obligation to your clients, what number are you? Why?

99

After you've discussed these questions with your candidate, you'll be able to ask yourself some additional, important questions:

5. Interpersonal Preferences
- What executive presence does the coach have? How

much confidence and hope does the coach generate? Why? How articulate, frank, and calm is the coach?

- Is the coach talking primarily to build rapport and trust or to win my business?
- How do I feel sitting and talking with the coach? Does the coach seem like a colleague? Friend? Detached expert? Salesperson? Collaborative problem-solver? Schmoozer?
- How well does the coach listen to me? Can the coach empathize with my feelings and grasp the thoughts behind my words?
- How comfortable would I feel in unloading or venting to the coach?
- What kind of sense of humor (if any) does the coach have and am I enjoying it? Self-deprecating? Sarcastic? Ingratiating?
- How forthcoming is the coach with me about the coach's professional ups, downs and challenges?
- How well do I think the coach has been developing professionally over the years?
- Is the coach constructively confrontational with me, asking direct questions and risking upsetting me, or is the coach anxious to be liked? Does the coach have the integrity to tell it to me straight even when I won't enjoy hearing it?
- What kind of chemistry do I seem to have with the coach? Why?

Weigh Your Findings

As you reflect on your notes, thoughts and feelings from the interviews, what makes any one candidate stand out from others? Is there a central theme for the coach or coaches you prefer? If you think a coaching candidate is exceptional, specifically how and why did you form this impression? What kind of partner would a candidate make during coaching? If you are considering multiple coaches, how are they most similar and most different from each other? What do you realistically anticipate in working with a coach, and why?

One suggestion I have for summarizing what you've learned in talking with a coach is to list what the coach's most significant strengths and weaknesses are in your opinion (see Appendix G). You could also once again compare the coaches' *TEC4* scores. How does one coach's list compare with those of other candidates? How would the strengths and weaknesses affect your coaching relationship and expected results, and why?

Driving Home

Let's consider a few of the many advantages you can exploit in Stage 2 and in closing out the evaluation and selection process. Collectively, these form a quality control sieve, putting you in control, washing out baloney and uncovering what's really going on. Specifically:

- You enter Stage 2 already well-versed in the candidate's work background—training, experience, education, and so on—giving you much more time in the interview to relax and look carefully at *the person* in front of you. No need to rush.
- You—not the candidate—drive the interview process. You refer anytime to your pick of 50+ suggested questions— plus any others important to you—that are penetrating. This means you not only set the *direction* of the discussion, but also the *depth*. You probe beyond glib or superficial answers until you're sure you see things clearly.
- Across the table, the candidate realizes pretty quickly that, rather than light-weight marshmallow inquiries anyone can answer and manipulate, your questions call for thoughtful, revealing responses demonstrating honesty, perspective and self-awareness—not to mention a full command of topics like

executive coaching.

- Once the ice is broken, small talk won't help the candidate much. She won't be asked to recite facts you already know (e.g. where she graduated or worked). Instead she'll be called to share thoughts, impressions, insights and feelings. She'll have the opportunity to be transparent with you which, by the way, is essential in building trust and coaching effectively. Your gut will tell you if this happens or not, so trust it.

- Realistically, your pointed probing into the candidate's intellect, emotions, self-awareness and leadership—over 90 minutes—doesn't leave the candidate with much room for dancing around issues or trying to charm you.

These are a few reasons, then, why the odds favor your emerging from Stage 2 with a sound, accurate understanding of your candidates. Thinking back to our five prototypes and particularly to our leading candidate coaches, Susan and Patricia, their particular similarities and differences would probably be much clearer to us after their interviews.

Payoff: The Informed, Accurate Choice

You're now armed with a comprehensive set of specific and helpful information about the executive coach or coaches who made it through Stage 1. You've digested the information and are well positioned for an astute choice. Instead of unknowingly skipping key questions or issues, missing important facts or relying too heavily on the feel of a coach, you can view each coach through several lenses. You'll be applying:

- Comparative, detailed data about specific and relevant qualifications in Stage 1 of the selection process. You've made wise first cuts based on knowledge of the candidates' backgrounds— saving substantial time and money and reducing risk.
- Systematic, organized impressions of each coach's intangible qualities using an interview organized so you can hone in on

five key areas—Stage 2 of the selection process and your analysis of each coach's performance in person.

- Confidence in the depth and breadth of the two-stage selection process, your final choice and the probability of an excellent return on your coaching investment.

- Opportunities for you to continue learning, sharing information, and further tuning your selection processes so future coaching choices provide even more value.

RECAP - CHAPTER 5

- You have evaluated and ranked candidate coaches using the *TEC4* in Stage 1 and made your first cut. Coaches whose *TEC4* results merit it move to Stage 2.

- Stage 2 centers around a 60-90 minute, face-to-face interview with coaches who made your first cut. This meeting can generate more objective information about a coach. Primarily, however, it's more subjective—giving you the chance to experience a coach and how he or she behaves and communicates.

- There are hundreds of characteristics and skills that are useful in the work of an executive coach. This list of qualities is so long that, instead of helping clarify the evaluation of coaches, it confuses the issue.

- Focus your interview around 5 characteristics of a coach. Sample questions are provided for you to use in learning more about each aspect of the coaches you interview.

- The 5 groups of characteristics have been widely-used for decades by psychiatrists, social workers, career counselors, psychologists and other occupational groups. They can help you gather more information about coaches you interview. They provide helpful lenses through which to view each candidate. These include 1) insight and self-aware-ness, 2) emotional and motivational qualities, 3) intellec-tual and problem-solving abilities, 4) leadership and man-agement styles and 5) interpersonal preferences.

- Suggestions are offered for you to use to help reflect back on your notes, thoughts, feelings and other impressions following the interviews. Processing this subjective infor-mation is important.

- You can use these interview results, together with the information generated in Stage 1 with the *TEC4*, to make a well-informed final choice of a coach. Your choice will be based on the synthesis of a full set of both objective and subjective information.

- This two-stage selection process helps you arrive at an excellent choice. It also provides rich feedback for coaches not selected—giving them a picture of strengths to build on and development areas to address.

Conclusion

LET'S WRAP THIS UP. WE'VE LOOKED AT HOW, AS AN INDUSTRY, EXECUTIVE COACH-ING HAS MADE LITTLE PROGRESS OVER THE PAST DECADES TO ORGANIZE AND STRUCTURE ITSELF TO SERVE AND PRO-TECT CONSUMERS. We know that a generally accepted set of comprehensive, global standards for executive coaching training, certification or licensure requirements is still not in place. The "Wild West" atmosphere consumers and practitioners face is fundamentally unchanged. Even in our most wildly optimistic moments, we don't expect the executive coaching industry to man-age itself any time soon. As consumers and motivated coaches, the buck stops with us. We're much more likely to successfully drive major upgrades in service quality and industry performance if we have thorough information and a selection process with teeth.

There has never been a requirement of any kind for becoming an executive coach. Anyone interested has and does offer executive coaching services. All these coaches create marketing messages in the hopes of convincing consumers to use their services. The resulting noise is confusing and frustrating for thousands of executives who simply want a reasonable and reliable way to identify the top-quality coach they need. As consumers, most of you simply do not have a full picture of what to look for and insist on in executive coaches, or of how to evaluate and compare coaches' most important characteristics. As motivated coaches, we don't have a comprehensive method for communicating value to clients, during both the hiring phase and the coaching relationship.

Our first assumption, based on both experience and common sense, is that outstanding executive coaches need considerable training, skill and experience to develop approaches and methodologies that are consistently successful. Our second assumption is that there are four fundamental areas in which quality executive coaches should demonstrate outstanding substance and depth: Business, Psychology, Coaching and Ethics.

In response to these assumptions, the *Top Executive Coach 4 (TEC4)* has been created. Its purpose is to help us compare executive coaches in the four fundamental categories. Data generated with the *TEC4* positions consumers to make a wise and informed first cut among executive coaches under consideration, saving significant time, money and other scarce resources. It provides coaches with objective feedback about why they are ultimately chosen or passed over. The *TEC4* can be used as is or adjusted based on your preferences and needs.

After making the first cut in Stage 1 of the evaluation process, we use sample questions (and others we prefer) in Stage 2 to learn more about any coaches still under consideration. In this second selection stage, interviewing the coaches in person is recommended, whenever possible. This gives us the chance to evaluate and understand the coaches from five perspectives: intellectual/problem-solving capacity, emotional/motivational qualities, interpersonal skills/impact, insight/self-awareness, and management/leadership approaches. Armed with both this subjective information and the more objective *TEC4* results, we can make meaningful distinctions between coaches and pick the strongest one.

This two-stage selection process is practical and carefully compares coaches with a comprehensive mix of objective data (e.g. business education and training) and subjective qualities (e.g. self-awareness). At the same time, it's relatively quick, efficient, systematic and thorough, focusing on key executive coaching success factors that are both factual and intangible.

Insight from Readers

The *TEC4* tool and the information we've covered here have resonated with business people, educators and coaches who have used it. It is my hope that it will improve your experiences with executive coaching and generate discussion and commentary from you. Your thoughtful feedback is invaluable and sincerely appreciated. The comments we received prior to publication are included in the Appendix and you'll find more at *www.pinpointingexcellence.com*.

Your engagement in the conversation, through feedback and more informed coaching choices, will translate into higher performance standards for the executive coaching industry and better results for consumers.

People who have pinpointed excellence in executive coaches by using the steps described here have been enthusiastic, finding their executive coaching choices more accurate, reliable and productive. Their additional feedback falls along the following lines:

No Guarantees

"There's not a 100% guarantee that every executive coach excellent in business, psychology, coaching and ethics will be the most effective with clients. Once in a while even the best-trained and qualified professional is not necessarily the most successful in working with clients."

This is true. We know excellence in education, training, experience and ongoing learning in any field does not necessarily guarantee the best client service. However, the reason so many professions have long ago worked to set these high standards is that excellence in these areas does maximize the probability of excellent preparation which, in turn, maximizes the probability of excellent performance and client service while minimizing the probability of substandard or damaging performance. In other words, standards of excellence are commonly and widely used in many professions because the standards help maintain service quality and protection for consumers.

Is There a Grandfather Clause for Experience?

"There are apparently a number of experienced executive coaches who would not be rated highly using your recommended selection process."

This is accurate and suggests a few points for us to consider. First, let's remember that years or even decades of 'executive coaching' experience initially based on partial or zero training and education is not exactly a success formula. At the same time, there are exceptions to every rule or norm. Second, the recommended selection process uncovers strengths and development opportunities for any coach, giving that coach the chance to further build knowledge and skill. Third, executives using the recommended selection process can effectively and specifically differentiate coaches based on strengths and development needs. Finally, if we were to hypothetically compare the effectiveness of, say, 2000 coaches rated low by the selection process and 2000 coaches rated high by the selection process, the differences in performance and quality between these groups can be expected to be both clear and substantial.

The selection process recommended in Pinpointing Excellence *is a leading-edge response to a situation all of us involved in the executive coaching industry need to address. While it is comprehensive, logical and based on both experience and the best of the standards currently available in the industry, it has not been in use long enough to generate extensive data on results. The* Top Executive Coach 4 *(TEC4) and the five suggested areas (and questions) to explore in interviewing a coach will continue to improve with future research.*

You Don't Know What I Really Value

"The selection process recommended in the book relies too heavily on a coach's training and education."

A coach's experience, training, education and continuing development are evaluated in Stage 1 of the recommended selection process. The goal is to minimize any bias based on training and education or experience or continuous development. In the first stage, using the TEC4 tool as recommended, the dimension of training and education is weighted equally with the dimension of applied experience.

"The selection process recommended in the book relies too heavily on a coach's experience."

A coach's experience, training, education and continuing development are evaluated in Stage 1 of the recommended selection process. The goal is to minimize any bias based on training and education or experience or continuous development. In the first stage, using the TEC4 tool as recommended, the dimension of applied experience is weighted equally with training and education.

"The selection process recommended in the book relies too heavily on subjective and intangible characteristics, particularly in the second stage."

Stage 2 of our selection process focuses on what we noted as the most important subjective and intangible characteristics in executive coaches. However, to minimize chances of you being overly dependent or singularly focused on these characteristics, Stage 2 is counterbalanced with Stage 1. In contrast with Stage 2, Stage 1 of the process centers on clarifying and evaluating more objective data with the TEC4 tool.

"It takes time and effort to assemble information about executive coach candidates if I follow the selection process recommended in the book."

Considering 1) the amount of money and time we invest in executive coaching and 2) the future impact of excellent vs. mediocre vs. poor results for individual clients and their organizations, any meaningful differences we can identify between excellence, mediocrity and poor quality in executive coaches have potentially huge consequences. Efforts we make in selecting executive coaches judiciously have excellent payoffs.

Benefits

The primary goal of this book is to maximize your success and effectiveness in evaluating, comparing, picking, engaging and generating excellent results with top-quality executive coaches. As you improve your results, you can reasonably expect more rapid executive development, increased profits, better than expected project success, and other improvements in your relevant key performance indicators.

I hope the book encourages you to stay on a learning path, continuously building skill in pinpointing the strongest and most productive executive coaches or in being that excellent coach. I encourage you to connect with friends and colleagues in and outside your organization to share your knowledge of the executive coaching industry and the effective practices you have come to expect.

It would be easy to underestimate the impact and power of each of your executive coaching choices. Actually, every sound, well-informed selection you make reverberates through the market. Executive coaches quickly notice. If you are a consumer, as you vote with your dollars, news of how you are increasingly knowledgeable and discriminating, and of how you go about making your coaching selections, will indeed travel—and <u>fast</u>.

Each of your selections can unmistakably boost (or lower) expectations and standards in the executive coaching industry. This not only helps you identify and use the top coaches available today. It also spurs training and development work by executive coaches who are recognizing how they need to improve to become or remain competitive. As the quality bar rises, the pool of outstanding executive coaches grows, benefiting all of us.

If you are a coach, the new quality standards you present to potential clients will become part of their expectations for every coach they encounter. We might also expect your desire to increase for high quality options in education and training since you will now be called by the market to account specifically for the quality and depth of your work experience, methodology, philosophy and knowledge. As other professionals have for years, executive coaches as a group will seek the strongest possible skill development, qualifications and credentials. This development, in turn,

111

should generate new and outstanding graduate programs in executive coaching at higher levels, including the doctoral level.

Looking ahead, we can picture executive coaches educated and trained in rigorous, highly selective graduate programs. These coaches would adhere to a single, demanding, globally recognized standard for service quality, certification and licensure. They would be well-grounded in coaching, of course, and also in business, psychology and ethics.

There would be consensus about what to expect in quality executive coaches. As these well-respected, skillful and responsible experts populate the marketplace, executive coaching at last would shift from 30 years of foggy permissiveness and become an exemplary profession.

Only by pinpointing excellence and then insisting on it can we expect to maximize the quality and benefits of executive coaching.

112

RECAP – CHAPTER 6

- Outstanding executive coaches need considerable training, skill and experience to develop approaches and methodologies that are consistently effective.

- Outstanding coaches also need considerable training, skill and experience in business, psychology, coaching and ethics.

- Many people who have applied the principles explained here and used the *TEC4* have shared their insights and enthusiasm. They have found their coaching selections more accurate, reliable and productive.

- Questions about the emphasis on education and training, applied experience or continuous development in the *TEC4* tool are addressed, including the relative weight given to education and training, applied experience, business depth and subjective factors. The ability of the two stage selection process to counter-balance each value and to offset objectivity and subjectivity is explained.

- *Pinpointing Excellence* was written in the hope that it would generate benefits including 1) maximizing consumer success and effectiveness in selecting a high quality executive coach, 2) encouraging continued learning and skill development in executive coach selections, 3) upgrading quality requirements in the executive coaching field with each savvy selection you make, 4) spurring training and development work by executive coaches who in rising numbers realize how they need to grow and improve just to be or to become competitive, and 5) increasing demand for rigorous and selective education and training programs in executive coaching.

113

Appendix

APPENDIX

First Response

Troy Thacker, Chief Executive Officer, R360 Environmental Solutions:
A terrific, easy to follow instruction manual for identifying, interviewing and selecting the right executive coach to fit your needs.

Dorothy Ables, Chief Administrative Officer, Spectra Energy:
The TEC4 tool and 2-stage process provide a useful model for the effective evaluation and selection of executive coaches. This increases the probability of successful coaching engagement outcomes. John's concepts are practical and thought provoking, and his recommended process is comprehensive, scalable and customizable, providing an appropriate blend of objective and subjective data points for selecting qualified coaches. Worth including in your toolkit.

Katie Mehnert, Global Behavioral Safety Program Manager, Shell:
Dr. Reed's book is an easy read for busy professionals and finally we have a practical, executable guide to finding a quality coach. *Pinpointing Excellence* is valuable for anyone: executives or rising leaders who need to secure the right coach. He cuts through the clutter and provides tools for getting the best outcome.

David Doll, Managing Director, Sequent Asset Management:
The volume of information available to executives is nearly limitless and is transmitted at incredible speed through and around an organization's leadership. The right executive coach acting as a sounding board, translator and content organizer has never been more important. *Pinpointing Excellence* provides a useful tool to help executives identify how the right coach gets them focused on the most important facets of their business and then makes sure they remain there.

Dave Massey, President, The REACH Group:
It's difficult to say who benefits most from Dr. Reed's work: those wanting a road map to become a highly effective executive coach; those needing to find the best matched executive coach to their organizational needs; or those in the executive coaching industry who as a whole are better off as this ground-breaking work boosts the qualifications bar in the coach selection process. All three groups will find the TEC4 tool logical, simple to understand, easy to wield and effective in matching executive coaches with coaching needs.

David LeVrier, Chief Administrative Officer, Hines:
Having for years been frustrated by the milieu of executive coaches in the market, I feel especially privileged and fortunate to not only have engaged John in successful coaching assignments for us at Hines, but also to experience first-hand his novel approach to equipping clients like me with a road map to be more effective in selecting coaches in the future. Businesses will benefit by finally having a clear standard in place to select practitioners of this crucial service, and having someone as qualified and capable as John help set that standard is a true Godsend for the industry.

Dr. Steve Currall, Dean and Professor of Management, Graduate School of Management, University of California, Davis:
I started reading *Pinpointing Excellence* and could not put it down. The book provides specific and actionable guidance for individuals seeking to find the ideal coach. This is exactly what the coaching community needs: a focus on what the consumer must know to make informed decisions about selecting a coach. Armed with this information, the person seeking a coaching relationship will make informed and precise judgments about choosing a coach, which will maximize the fit between the coach and his or her advisee. Finding a great fit is the key to a maximally effective work relationship.

117

Richard Davis, Managing Director, Canaccord Genuity:
Clearly a wake-up call for executive coaches and their clients. *Pinpointing Excellence* concisely delivers a practical prescription for those planning to engage an executive coach while also providing a path to recovery for an industry that is sleepwalking into crisis. I'm recommending this book to software CEO's, board members and leading venture investors.

Dr. Billie Blair, President and Chief Executive Officer, Change Strategists, Inc. and Author, Value Plus: Employees as Valuers:
At last! A clear depiction of what can be gained from hiring an executive coach combined with excellent guidance on selection. Dr. Reed has developed a straightforward coaching assessment process in conjunction with a good explanation of how to choose the right professional. This achievement represents a strong step forward for the executive coaching field and offers welcome support for executives initiating a coaching selection process.

Dr. John Eliot, Author, Overachievement and Consultant, Stanford University:

Dr. Reed's executive coaching wisdom is second to none. There is no one better to lead the way in developing immensely needed evaluation tools for the field. Before you hire a coach, read this book!

Dr. Tom West, Vice Chair, Northside Anesthesiology:

After reading this book, I'm clear about why it's imperative to evaluate and pick executive coaches based on relevant qualifications. I'm responsible for evaluating my physician colleagues' effectiveness. It's obvious now that, while colleagues offer themselves as "executive coaches," their actual qualifications vary drastically. The TEC4 helps sift out coaches with specific levels of education, experience and skill and I now insist on depth in business, psychology, coaching and ethics. Looking back, I see how easily we fall prey to picking coaches based on personal chemistry or gut feelings. John cautions that this wastes precious time and money while usually failing to generate the best available coaching candidate. He offers practical examples and sample questions to help us assess coaches thoroughly. I now have specific, executable steps and tools for improving my organization. If that's your goal, I highly recommend this book.

Richard Thayer, Founder, Rich-Change Consulting:

Activity in executive coaching as a recognizable specialty has exploded in recent years. Dr. Reed's new book *Pinpointing Excellence* comes at an ideal time for those tasked with identifying and selecting executive coaches. The book will reward even the busiest of executives who can dip into it enough to glean the importance of using clear quantitative and qualitative criteria in their selection.

Dr. David Bracken, Vice President, OrgVitality, LLC:

The explosion of executive coaching makes *Pinpointing Excellence* an important resource for coaches, coaches in training, leaders in search of a coach, and HR professionals supporting leadership development functions. Dr. Reed's TEC4 is a prescription for successful executive coaches and a diagnostic process – and it allows for the necessary flexibility to accommodate unique needs of potential coaching clients. If widely adopted, *Pinpointing Excellence* will move the executive coaching profession ahead in a quantum leap.

Dr. Robert Perkins, President, Corporate Psychology and Professor, Stetson School of Business and Economics, Mercer University:

Dr. Reed's book *Pinpointing Excellence* fills a vital gap in the executive coaching field. His clear and conversational tone makes this groundbreaking guide easy reading. More importantly, his recommendations reflect an expert overview of potential problems companies will encounter when hiring executive coaches. He offers a brilliant framework with practical methods to address the issues. His insights are rooted in deep experience and understanding of both the range of coaches, many of whom will have serious flaws that the unwary would not detect, and consumers' difficulties in making excellent selections in this growing but "wild and wooly" market. If there is a shortcoming, it is only that the book is too short. We hope a second edition will add even more examples to give neophytes greater perspective on how to evaluate answers to Dr. Reed's probing questions for "would be" coaches. On balance, this is an outstanding, pioneering work, a "must read" for all those interested in the challenging field of executive development.

Christa Tillman, Manager, KPMG:

Dr. Reed takes an insightful look at the executive coaching industry and calls on both consumers and practitioners to raise the bar. He simultaneously challenges practicing coaches and those considering hiring coaches to apply thorough and relevant analyses to make an informed decision. By effectively arming consumers with the TEC4 tool, he's leveled the playing field to ensure they do not simply rely on intangibles or a "gut feeling" to make a decision. This evaluative process provides the basis for a productive coaching relationship and ensures ROI for the client.

119

Dr. Braden Allenby, Professor, Engineering and Ethics,
Arizona State University:

Executive coaching has become an important element of competitive success for many individuals and firms, and a large and growing area of practice in its own right. John's *Pinpointing Excellence* has caught executive coaching at its inflexion point, where it can no longer justify the lack of standards and the informal processes that have characterized its early development, and must begin moving towards a more structured professionalism. His critique of the status quo is acute, and his suggestion of a method, TEC4, to accelerate development of standards of practice and professionalism in this important area is a welcome innovation.

Kenneth Hall, Director, Deutsche Bank Americas:

The financial services industry has seen an increasing need for executive coaching in recent years as institutions have struggled with massive dislocation and market change. In this book, Dr. Reed provides a detailed methodology for identifying and selecting high quality coaches who have the training, experience and insights to address this need. Executives and organizations of all kinds should find this methodology highly useful in finding coaches who will be able to meet their specific requirements.

Todd Greenwalt, Attorney-at-Law:

As someone with little experience choosing an executive coach, I found *Pinpointing Excellence* to be a straightforward explanation of the coaching profession and the expectations clients should have when engaging an executive coach. Moreover, the TEC4 evaluation process is easy to understand and presents a systematic approach for selecting an executive coach. Direct and concise, *Pinpointing Excellence* helps even a layperson gain the tools necessary to confidently evaluate and select an executive coach.

Kimball Kehoe, D.B.A., Senior Lecturer in Management, Jones Graduate School of Business, Rice University:

Selecting a coach for a top executive is a high risk activity. For one thing, there are several factors to consider. For another, it is usually a one-shot, hit or miss and the costs of a miss are high: frustration, wasted time and money, and a lower reputation for the coach. *Pinpointing Excellence* provides a selection process that greatly improves the chances of success. In the first stage, coaches are evaluated according to four relevant categories. This ensures that consumers are not taken in by smooth-talking, questionably-qualified coaches. The second stage calls for a face-face conversation, an interactive basis for judging how well the consumer and coach will work together. The combination of these two evaluation stages greatly improves the odds of creating a productive match. Time and effort going into the selection is minor compared to the value of the executive's improved performance.

Mark Worscheh, Executive Vice President, Aquinas Companies, LLC:

Executive coaching has rapidly emerged as a critical development tool for organizations seeking to leverage their substantial investment in senior managers. Now, Dr. Reed presents a useful methodology for screening and evaluating coaching professionals, offering a disciplined program to replace what for many consumers is a haphazard hiring process. Moreover, the TEC4 serves as an ideal guide for the industry, providing a professional development framework for coaching practitioners seeking excellence in their field.

Dr. Tom Pace, Senior Pastor, St. Luke's United Methodist Church:

The right coach can be a transformative influence on a leader, helping him or her achieve both personal and organizational goals. But if the coach is a bad fit for the expressed need, the experience is both frustrating and counterproductive. John provides an excellent tool in the TEC4 to clarify both the needs of the client and the abilities and strengths of a coach. We use executive coaches often in our organization and, from here on out, we'll use *Pinpointing Excellence* every time we choose one.

Frank Donnelly, President, Wärtsilä North America, Inc.:
Don't hire an executive coach before reading *Pinpointing Excellence*. The success of a coaching engagement depends on the coach's relevant training and experience, and a proper match with the executive. The TEC4 tool offers a simple, step-by-step process for evaluating and selecting the most appropriate coach. Maximize your executive coaching results by applying these recommended methods in your search.

Lauri Lipka, Director, Global Talent Management, AGCO Corporation:
Our world is ever-changing and how we lead is no different. Great leaders adapt and inspire others to reach their highest potential. For many in our organization, this is not an area of expertise so we often rely on executive coaches for our key leaders to provide them with critical feedback and support for long-term success. This is not an investment to be taken lightly – nor should the selection of executive coaches. This is why the information in *Pinpointing Excellence* is invaluable: a well thought out framework and clear guidance on how to identify and select the best coach possible. Follow this advice and you'll be well on your way to building a strong leadership pipeline.

Jim Campbell, Host, "Business Talk with Jim Campbell" on Yale
Broadcasting and the Business Talk Radio Network:
Rare is the book that transforms an industry. John has developed executive coaching best practices to upgrade the field to a level of excellence and quality control consistent with medicine, law and accounting. With an MBA from Dartmouth, a PhD in psychology from the University of Georgia and 30 years of experience, he brings both business and behavioral perspectives to the executive coaching world. *Pinpointing Excellence* is a must read before engaging a coach. With an easy-to-use tool (TEC4), John focuses on the quality, qualifications, and ethics coaches must bring to the table. He's the "executive coach" of executive coaches.

Jamie Belinne, SPHR, Assistant Dean, Rockwell Career Center,
Bauer College, University of Houston:
There's a frightening lack of standards for executive coaches today while increasingly individuals and corporations recognize the link between quality coaching and professional success. *Pinpointing Excellence* gives specific tools, insight and steps to help us cut through the hype and hire the most qualified and effective coaches for our needs. I work with so many executives who want to take their careers to the next level. Unfortunately some don't realize until too late that inadequately-trained coaches can do more career damage than good. I highly recommend applying the resources in *Pinpointing Excellence* before considering a long-term coaching relationship with anyone.

Mike Feinberg, Co-Founder, KIPP:
We know failure is a key ingredient of success but if we don't learn from our failures, ingredients won't help if they remain on the shelf. In *Pinpointing Excellence*, John Reed helps us understand why executive coaching can be so helpful in learning more about ourselves, our successes and failures, and how finding the right coach is vital and both an art and a science.

Bradford Agry, Founding Principal, CareerTeam Partners:
Selecting the best possible executive coach is an often confusing process for any consumer – line managers, HR managers and individuals. In an unlicensed field with no clear-cut or standardized metrics of excellence, John Reed has provided an imminently readable and tightly written book. *Pinpointing Excellence* leads buyers through a practical and methodical process to narrow down and make wise coach selections. Looking at candidate coaches through the lens of four dimensions (business, psychological, coaching and ethical depth) is a new and creative means of cutting to the chase – answering the question "Is this person the best possible match for my needs?" I hope people on all sides of our field use this valuable evaluation tool regularly.

Mary Grace Gray, General Manager, Hotel GRANDUCA:
I was totally immersed in this book. It is compelling. Simply put, *Pinpointing Excellence* is a great read for anyone contemplating working with an executive coach.

Dr. Thomas Horvath, Professor, Menninger Department of Psychiatry, Baylor College of Medicine and Retired Chief of Staff, DeBakey Veterans Administration Medical Center:
As a neuropsychiatrist and healthcare executive who has been critical of the vagueness in the field of organizational management, I found Dr. Reed's book *Pinpointing Excellence* a breath of fresh air. His structured, evidence based, value focused work on executive coaches should bring some order into their growing field. The approach he so clearly describes can be usefully adapted to other hiring or promotion decisions that human service or business organizations employ. The reality is that we all need to pinpoint true excellence instead of having the Peter Principle or buddy favoritism dominate our

Dave Guerra, Chief Executive Officer, Corpus Optima:
Pinpointing Excellence is an important, critical contribution, and much needed guidance. John Reed is bringing executive coaching into the 21st Century.

Rakhee Das, Vice President, Teledata:
Pinpointing Excellence is a wonderful and important read for leaders reaching a stage when mere management skills are no longer enough to build a business. Increasingly we turn to coaches to help us be more effective, fine tune our skills and understand our challenges. Only well-trained, confident and skilled coaches can successfully address an executive's limitations while energizing strengths. Most of us don't follow clear, structured guidelines to identify a coach. As a remedy, *Pinpointing Excellence* empowers us, the buyers, to make knowledgeable and consequential choices in searching for the 'right' coach. John Reed's book is timely and relevant in a growing marketplace where leaders seek benefits of quality coaching but lack the judgment, intelligibility, and know-how to pick the best person for the job.

John Godbold, President, Houston Energy Associates, LLC:
Without standards or accreditation for becoming an executive coach and without consumers having a systematic approach for evaluating coaches, choosing a coach is precarious and likely done on a superficial, qualitative basis. As an engineer, I see why this produces so many problems. Dr. Reed's analytical tool (TEC4) appeals to me as a disciplined, structured and logical means of evaluating candidate coaches. There's an unwavering focus on all key criteria for executive coaching effectiveness: business, psychological, coaching, and ethical depth. *Pinpointing Excellence* is a must have resource – a realistic, step by step manual for the critical task of selecting the top executive coach.

123

Kenneth E. McKay, Partner, Locke Lord Bissell & Liddell LLP:
Pinpointing Excellence targets a previously unaddressed phenomenon—the lack of any peer accepted standard for defining executive coaches—and pragmatically presents a systematic but pliable solution. By providing thoughtful criteria for identifying a coach qualified and suited to tackle an entity's particular goals, the *TEC4* offers a universally applicable guide to the coach selection process without being generic. Rather, Reed's potent methodology allows executives to accentuate client-specific priorities and values to tailor the search and the ultimate coach selection. This book is a must read for any business contemplating retaining an executive coach, and a shot across the bow aimed at an industry apparently otherwise content to hit the snooze alarm.

Bibliography

Academy of Management, www.aomonline.org

Anderson, M., & Escher, P., *The MBA Oath: Setting a Higher Standard for Business Leaders* (New York: Portfolio, 2010).

Berglas, S., "The Very Real Dangers of Executive Coaching," *Harvard Business Review, June, 2002*, 86-92.

Bresser, F., "Frank Bresser Consulting Report: Executive Summary – Global Coaching Survey 2008/2009", (Cologne: Frank Bresser Consulting, July 2009)

Coaching and Mentoring: How to Develop Top Talent and Achieve Stronger Performance. (Boston: Harvard Business Press, 2004).

Coutu, D., & Kauffman, C. "What Coaches Can Do for You." *HBR Research Report, January, 2009*, 91-97.

Coutu, D., & Kauffman, C. "The Realities of Executive Coaching," *HBR Research Report, January, 2009*, 1-32.

Ennis, S., Goodman, R., Hodgetts, W., Hunt, J., Mansfield, R., Otto, J., et al., *Core Competencies of the Executive Coach*, (The Executive Coaching Forum, 2005).

Grahek, M. S., Thompson, A. D., & Toliver, A. "The Character to Lead: A Closer Look at Character in Leadership." *Consulting Psychology Journal, (62)* 2010, 270-290.

iCoachNewYork, www.icoachnewyork.com

International Association of Coaching, www.certifiedcoach.org

International Coach Federation, www.coachfederation.org

International Consortium for Coaching in Organizations, www.coachingconsortium.org

Kilburg, R. R., *Executive Coaching: Developing Managerial Wisdom in a World of Chaos*, (Washington: American Psychological Association, 2000).

Kilburg, R. R., *Executive Wisdom: Coaching and The Emergence of Virtuous Leaders*, (Washington: American Psychological Association, 2006).

Levine, M., "Choosing an Executive Coach: Speed Dating or an Arranged Marriage?" *The Linkage Leader, 1*, 2008, 1-3.

LinkedIn, www.linkedin.com

Michelman, P., "Methodology: Do you need an executive coach?" *Harvard Management Update*, *9* (12), 2004 , 2-3.

Morgan, H., Harkins, P., and Goldsmith, M. *The Art and Practice of Leadership Coaching: 50 Top Executive Coaches Reveal Their Secrets*, (Hoboken: John Wiley & Sons, 2005).

NCS Pearson, Inc., *Watson-Glaser Critical Thinking Appraisal* (Copyright 2007)

Peltier, B., *The Psychology of Executive Coaching*, (New York: Routledge, 2010).

Personnel Today, www.personneltoday.com

Scoular, P., "How Do You Pick a Coach?" *HBR Research Report*, January, 2009. 96.

Sherman, S., & Freas, A., "The Wild West of Executive Coaching," *Harvard Business Review*, November 2004, 82-90.

Sidle, S., "Personality Disorders and Dysfunctional Employee Behavior: How Can Managers Cope?" *Academy of Management Perspectives*, *25*, May, 2011, 76-77.

The Executive Coaching Handbook: Principles and Guidelines for a Successful Coaching Partnership. *The Executive Coaching Forum*, November 2008 (4th Edition).

Thompson, A. D., Grahek, M., Phillips, R. E., & Fay, C. L., "The Search for Worthy Leadership," *Consulting Psychology Journal, (60)*, 2008, 366-382.

Worldwide Association of Business Coaches, www.wabccoaches.com

125

Acknowledgments

THANKS FOR THIS BOOK go first to the executives who for years have trusted me to enter their lives and organizations and, in the process, to learn and develop. Your challenges, intelligence, insights, openness, courage and resilience fuel the good work we do together.

Thanks to the educators and other leaders from Deerfield Academy, Dartmouth College, The Tuck School of Business at Dartmouth, Georgia State University and the University of Georgia who modeled strong ethics, fine character and passion for critical thinking and clear writing.

Thanks to Lucy Chambers, Ellen Cregan and the Bright Sky Press team for their skill, perspective and warmth in the publishing process. This book's quality stems in large part from your keen eyes and judgment.

Thanks to the great friends and colleagues who over decades have so graciously shared their understanding, encouragement, wisdom and talent to help me in countless moments and ways.

Thanks to my parents Lansing and Kate, my sisters Martha and Katherine, my brother Matthew, my aunt Martia and my uncle Mark, my in laws Richard and Sally, my brothers in law Richard and Clark, and their families—your love and support give meaning and happiness beyond anything possible to write here.

Thanks to Alison, Elisabeth, Haley and Chase for the marvelous moments of being a dad, for the pride and excitement you generate, and for the love we will always share.

Thanks to my wife Perry Ann, the most extraordinary mix of love, wisdom, talent, courage, leadership and beauty, for helping me appreciate all we're blessed with and what really matters in our life together.

Finally, and most important, thanks to God for opportunities to use skills He alone provides and for leading me to this chance to help others, I trust, according to His will.

The following appendices are offered to help you get rolling with the evaluation and selection process. You're welcome to reproduce or otherwise use this information as needed. However, since this information is proprietary, please have the following text appear legibly on each page, slide, or other form of material you distribute or otherwise use:

Copyright © 2011 by Dr. John L. Reed. All rights reserved.
www.pinpointingexcellence.com

APPENDIX A – STANDARD *TEC4* WORKSHEET

1. Business Depth
- Applied Experience   0-10 points   ____
- Education & Training   0-10 points   ____
- Continuous Development   0-5 points   ____

2. Psychology Depth
- Applied Experience   0-10 points   ____
- Education & Training   0-10 points   ____
- Continuous Development   0-5 points   ____

3. Coaching Depth
- Applied Experience   0-10 points   ____
- Education & Training   0-10 points   ____
- Continuous Development   0-5 points   ____

4. Ethics Depth
- Business Ethics Code*   0-5 points   ____
- Psychology Ethics Code**   0-5 points   ____
- Coaching Ethics Code***   0-15 points   ____

          TOTAL   0-100 points   ____

Academy of Management, for instance

**American Psychological Association, for instance*

***Worldwide Association of Business Coaches, for instance*

Copyright © 2011 by Dr. John L. Reed. All rights reserved. www.pinpointingexcellence.com

APPENDIX B – INTELLECTUAL/PROBLEM SOLVING ABILITIES

- How do you think, analyze issues, reach solutions and solve problems? Are you more logical than intuitive, or vice-versa? Why?
- Explain your methods. Why are they effective? (Note of how clearly the candidate answers.)
- What level(s) of executives (e.g. entry level managers, C-level leaders) do you brainstorm or problem-solve with? Examples?
- What is your knowledge and experience level in my industry?
- Tell me how you've experienced challenges and issues varying with clients in different organizational roles at different levels?
- How do you apply your expertise in business, psychology, coaching and ethics in working with clients? Examples?
- How flexible are you as a thinker and problem solver? How open are you to others' ideas?
- Do you use any particular coaching methods? Why?
- How do you learn about new concepts or findings in your field? Examples?
- How do you work to add to your knowledge of, for example, business, psychology, coaching and ethics? Examples?

NOTES

Copyright © 2011 by Dr. John L. Reed. All rights reserved. www.pinpointingexcellence.com

APPENDIX C – EMOTIONAL CHARACTERISTICS

- What are you passionate about?
- What drives you? What are your priorities?
- How resilient and persistent are you in the face of obstacles to goals? Examples?
- How well do you tolerate stress? Examples?
- How direct, open and transparent are you with feelings and thoughts?
- What makes you happy? Frustrated? Distracted? Excited?
- How would a person know how you're feeling?
- What's your motivation as a coach? Is it to build your client's skills and success or to become a support? Why?
- What are you most proud of? Why?

NOTES

Copyright © 2011 by Dr. John L. Reed. All rights reserved. www.pinpointingexcellence.com

APPENDIX D – INSIGHT

- How do you view yourself? (How close is this coach's view to what you are seeing? Why?)
- How well do you understand your own biases? How do you compensate for them in working with clients? Examples?
- What important points or events in life contributed to your development? How? Why?
- Who do you aspire to be as an exceptional, best-in-class executive coach? Why?
- What would people who know you well say are your top 3-5 strengths? Worst 3-5 weaknesses? Why?
- How helpful or challenging would your strengths and weaknesses be for me as your client?
- Can you provide a fresh perspective on my situation and goals? Why?
- How do you learn about the people around you? How do you adjust to them? Examples?
- What have been the most important professional and personal experiences for you? Why?
- If you waved a magic wand and became perfect, what would change about you? Why?
- What was your ideal of excellent coaching when you began work as a coach? How (if at all) has this ideal changed over the years? Why?

NOTES

Copyright © 2011 by Dr. John L. Reed. All rights reserved. www.pinpointingexcellence.com

APPENDIX E – LEADERSHIP / WORK STYLE

- What's your style working with clients? Motivating? Open? Frank? Organized? Informal? Demanding? Authoritative? Global or linear?
- What is your role in empowering and developing others?
- If 10 means efficient micromanager and 0 means excellent delegator, what number are you? Why? What was your number a decade ago? Why?
- Are you a glass half full or half empty person? Why?
- How bottom-line and decisive are you? How much do you make suggestions and then expect the client to decide? Examples?
- What are your ethical responsibilities to your clients?
- What are your thoughts on how adults learn and grow? How do you encourage and facilitate adult growth and behavior change?
- How do you plan work and manage the relationship with the client?
- How practical vs. theoretical or conceptual are you? How well do you see your approach fitting my situation? Why?
- What are your biggest challenges in working with clients?
- Do you feel that you are more respected or appreciated by your clients?
- Is your work-style based more on 'steak' (e.g. substantive knowledge and skill) or 'sizzle' (e.g. pep-talks, cheerleading)? Why?
- If 10 means you absolutely loving your work and 0 means you do it out of a sense of obligation to your clients, what number are you? Why?

NOTES

Copyright © 2011 by Dr. John L. Reed. All rights reserved. www.pinpointingexcellence.com

APPENDIX F – INTERPERSONAL PREFERENCES

- What executive presence does the coach have? How much confidence and hope does the coach generate? Why? How articulate, frank, and calm is the coach?
- Is the coach talking with me primarily to build rapport and trust or to win my business?
- How do I feel sitting and talking with the coach? Does the coach seem like a colleague? Friend? Detached expert? Salesperson? Collaborative problem-solver? Schmoozer?
- How well does the coach listen to me? Can the coach empathize with my feelings or grasp the thoughts behind my words?
- How comfortable would I feel in unloading or venting to the coach?
- What sense of humor (if any) does the coach have and am I enjoying it? Self-deprecating? Sarcastic? Ingratiating? Does it mesh with mine?
- How forthcoming is the coach with me about professional ups, downs and challenges?
- How do I think the coach has been developing professionally over the years? Personally?
- Is the coach constructively confrontational with me, asking direct questions and risking upsetting me—or is the coach anxious to be liked? Does the coach have the integrity to tell it to me straight even if I won't enjoy hearing it?
- What kind of chemistry do I seem to have with the coach? Why?

NOTES

Copyright © 2011 by Dr. John L. Reed. All rights reserved. www.pinpointingexcellence.com

APPENDIX G - ASSESSMENT SUMMARY

CANDIDATE NAME: _____

STAGE 1 - *TEC4* SCORE:_____

TEC4 STRENGTHS   *TEC4* GAPS

STAGE 2 – INTERVIEW RESULTS:

INTELLECTUAL/PROBLEM-SOLVING ABILITY
STRENGTHS   **GAPS**

EMOTIONAL CHARACTERISTICS
STRENGTHS   **GAPS**

INSIGHT
STRENGTHS   **GAPS**

LEADERSHIP/WORK STYLE
STRENGTHS   **GAPS**

INTERPERSONAL PREFERENCES
STRENGTHS   **GAPS**

Copyright © 2011 by Dr. John L. Reed. All rights reserved. www.pinpointingexcellence.com

APPENDIX H – *TEC4* SCORING GUIDES

Applied Experience (Business) (0 – 10 points):

- 20+ yrs. of top quality experience   10 points
- 20+ yrs. of solid quality experience   8-9 points
- 11-19 yrs. of top quality experience   6-7 points
- 11-19 yrs. of solid quality experience   5 points
- 5-10 yrs. of top quality experience   4 points
- 5-10 yrs. of solid quality experience   3 points
- 1-4 yrs. of top quality experience   2 points
- 1-4 yrs. of solid quality experience   1 point

Education & Training (Business) (0 – 10 points):

- Top 25 MBA Program   9-10 points
- Selective MBA Program   7-8 points
- Non-selective MBA Program   5-6 points
- Bachelor's Degree Program   2-4 points
- Associate's Degree Program   0-1 point

Continuous Development (Business)(0-5 points):

- Regular, documented learning   5 points
- Occasional, documented learning   1-2 points
- No documented learning   0 points

Applied Experience (Psychology) (0-10 points):

- 20+ yrs. of top quality experience   10 points
- 20+ yrs. of solid quality experience   8-9 points
- 11-19 yrs. of top quality experience   6-7 points
- 11-19 yrs. of solid quality experience   5 points
- 5-10 yrs. of top quality experience   4 points
- 5-10 yrs. of solid quality experience   3 points
- 1-4 yrs. of top quality experience   2 points
- 1-4 yrs. of solid quality experience   1 point

Education & Training (Psychology) (0-10 points):

- Doctoral degree, licensure Top 25 program   10 points
- Doctoral degree, licensure selective program   8-9 points
- Doctoral degree, licensure non-select program   6-7 points
- Master's degree, Top 25 program   5 points
- Master's degree, selective program   4 points
- Master's degree, non-selective program   3 points

Copyright © 2011 by Dr. John L. Reed. All rights reserved. www.pinpointingexcellence.com

- Bachelor's degree program — 1-2 points
- Associate's degree program — 0-1 points

Continuous Development (Psychology) (0- 5 points):
- Regular, documented learning — 5 points
- Occasional, documented learning — 1-2 points
- No documented learning — 0 points

Applied Experience (Coaching)(0-10 points):
- 2000+ documented coaching hours — 10 points
- 1500+ documented coaching hours — 8-9 points
- 1000+ documented coaching hours — 6-7 points
- 500+ documented coaching hours — 4-5 points
- 1+ documented coaching hours — 0-3 points

Education & Training (Coaching)(0-10 points):
- Master's degree accredited program — 10 points
- Quality certification (e.g. WABC) program — 8-9 points
- Lesser quality certification program — 1-7 points
- No graduate education or certification — 0 points

Continuous Development (Coaching) (0-5 points):
- Regular, documented learning — 5 points
- Occasional, documented learning — 1-2 points
- No documented learning — 0 points

Business Ethics Code (0-5 points):
- Adhere to documented ethics code — 5 points
- No documented ethics code — 0 points

Psychology Ethics Code (0-5 points):
- Adhere to documented ethics code — 5 points
- No documented ethics code — 0 points

Coaching Ethics Code (0-15 points):
- Adhere to documented ethics code — 15 points
- No documented ethics code — 0 points

Copyright © 2011 by Dr. John L. Reed. All rights reserved. www.pinpointingexcellence.com